dear sister

letters from survivors of sexual violence

Edited by
Lisa Factora-Borchers

"Reading *Dear Sister*, I felt like I was sitting in a circle and each time I turned a page, a woman stepped forward—with a letter or an interview or a drawing or an essay or a poem—and she knew exactly how I felt and she could see me and she understood. This book offers us that: the juxtaposition of being visible and still being safe, the *cariño* of women speaking directly to us, not at us. Each page is an affirmation: the world does truly have so much love to offer and so much care."—Daisy Hernández, coeditor, *Colonize This! Young Women of Color on Today's Feminism*

"A much-needed counterweight to the all-too-prevalent victim-blaming and shaming, every person should have a copy of *Dear Sister* on their shelves so that they can reach out and support their friends in times of need."—Vikki Law, author and activist, *Resistance Behind Bars: The Struggles Of Incarcerated Women* and *Don't Leave Your Friends Behind: Concrete Ways to Support Families in Social Justice Movements*

"This chilling, heartbreaking, and necessary collection consists of letters from 40 artists, activists, writers, and students, who are survivors of sexual assault and here offer counsel to "sister" survivors. Every story is shadowed by the teller's sense of shame, brokenness, depression, and pain, but at the same time, in anticipation of the addressees' experience of sexual assault, the letters also offer comfort, solidarity, reassurance, the possibility of healing, and testimony of survival. Unquestionably moving."—*Publishers Weekly*

dear
sister

letters from survivors of sexual violence

Edited by
Lisa Factora-Borchers

Foreword by
Aishah Shahidah Simmons

AK
PRESS
EDINBURGH • OAKLAND • BALTIMORE

Dear Sister:
Letters from Survivors of Sexual Violence
Edited by Lisa Factora-Borchers

© 2014 Lisa Factora-Borchers
This edition © 2014 AK Press (Edinburgh, Oakland, Baltimore)

ISBN: 978-1-84935-172-0
e-ISBN: 978-1-84935-173-7
Library of Congress Control Number: 2013945490

AK Press	AK Press UK
674-A 23rd Street	PO Box 12766
Oakland, CA 94612	Edinburgh EH8 9YE
USA	Scotland
www.akpress.org	www.akuk.com
akpress@akpress.org	ak@akedin.demon.co.uk

The above addresses would be delighted to provide you with
the latest AK Press distribution catalog, which features several
thousand books, pamphlets, zines, audio and video recordings, and
gear, all published or distributed by AK Press. Alternately, visit our
websites to browse the catalog and find out
the latest news from the world of anarchist publishing:
www.akpress.org | www.akuk.com
revolutionbythebook.akpress.org

Printed in the United States on recycled, acid-free paper.

Cover by Kate Khatib | www.manifestor.org/design
Interior by Margaret Killjoy | www.birdsbeforethestorm.net
Back cover image by Favianna Rodriguez | www.favianna.com

TABLE OF CONTENTS

*This book is dedicated to all those
living with and healing from
memories of sexual violence.*

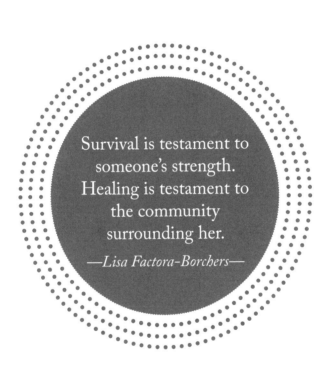

Survival is testament to someone's strength. Healing is testament to the community surrounding her.

—*Lisa Factora-Borchers*—

Aishah Shahidah Simmons

One cannot choose to be raped.
But one can choose to survive.

When I first read the precious gift that you have in your hands, Dear Reader, I reflected upon a profound Dear Sister moment on my life's journey, which took place in 1989. It wasn't a letter, but rather a conversation between two college sophomore friends.

Upon my return home to Philadelphia from my first trip to Mexico on a study abroad program, I was terrified that I might be pregnant. I disclosed about the journey that led to my pregnancy fear to one of my dearest friends, Marielle, who was interning at Women Organized Against Rape (WOAR). I shared with her that I paid for the hotel room where I had sex with a man. I told her that while I initially said yes to our having sex, I changed my mind once I got into our dank, nasty hotel room and told him I didn't want to do it. He completely ignored my expressed wish not to have sex. He forced me to have sex against my will. At that time, in my mind's eye, it wasn't brutal because I said *no* and he said *yes*. I didn't know that *no*s could and should be respected. I didn't attempt to physically fight him because I was afraid and I knew I had to wait until the morning to return to university student housing.

I was afraid because I had already broken all of the rules by sneaking to be with him, and my girlfriends were covering for me. I didn't want to get them or myself in trouble, so I just acquiesced to his wishes. The following morning I reconnected with my friends and other classmates. I lied to my friends who were waiting to hear a "good" sex story. I told them I had a great time, which was anything but true. Later that day, I met another man and had very pleasurable, consensual sex with him. Hindsight tells me that I wanted to reclaim my body and my sexuality. At the time, however, I thought I was being a "slut" (whatever that means), and I was ashamed of my behavior.

Upon hearing my story, Marielle was adamant that the first time was rape and that nothing was wrong with my having consensual sex with another man the next night. I thought she was out of her mind. Rape doesn't happen when you say yes and then change your mind. Rape doesn't happen when you pay for the hotel room. No, that's not rape, I thought and even said. I told her I was indecisive and probably led him on by my mixed message. I honestly thought Marielle had taken her internship at WOAR way too seriously, to the point that she had lost touch with the fact that rape is when a strange, unidentifiable man in the bushes, hallway, or streets attacks you and violates your body at gun- or knifepoint. Part of me thought she had gone off the deep end. This was not the case, of course. She knew exactly what she was talking about, and whenever we talked she compassionately would not allow me to blame myself for the trauma that I endured.

I did become pregnant, and I was unsure which man—the one who raped me or the one with whom I had pleasurable, consensual sex the night after my rape—was the father. I believe that it's important, for those who are able, to share our complex sexual herstories, which are often a mixture of trauma and pleasure. Marielle went with me to the Elizabeth Black Health Center for Women on the day of my abortion. This is not something that I take lightly or even write easily, because I believe in the sanctity of all life and I'm vehemently pro-choice. I want a world where all Beings everywhere and without exception are free and safe from enmity and danger, and are well nurtured, loved, peaceful, and happy. When I think about the frightened twenty-year-old Aishah on that day in April 1989, I know that I was in no position to carry out the powerful responsibility of being a mother. Even if I were in a position to be, I'm certain that it was the right decision for me at that time.

Marielle and I crossed the vitriolic anti-reproductive justice protestors together to get inside of the building. Even though she wasn't allowed to be with me for most of the day, she waited at the center until I was discharged approximately six hours later. Marielle had a bouquet of flowers in her hand and told me that I was beautiful and courageous. In spite of my belief at the time that she had no idea what rape was, I am forever grateful to Marielle Joy Cohen for planting the seed that transformed into a tree of survivorship. She will always hold a special place in my heart. It wasn't until three years later that I began the twenty-one-years-and-counting work through therapy with a Black feminist licensed clinical psychologist, anti-rape activism, cultural work, and vipassana meditation as taught by S.N. Goenka to both heal myself and support the healing of others.

When I read and then reread the masterPEACE that you, Dear Reader, are holding in your hands, I was reminded that I am not alone. I am a part of a mosaic of diverse individuals whose herstories, histories, and contemporary realities are different, and yet we share a commonality of moving from victim to survivor.

Dear Sister: Letters to Survivors of Sexual Violence is both a sacred and transformative collage of non-linear road maps to survival and healing. It is an unconditional love offering from and to survivors. It is a powerful tool for allies, even those who want but don't how to be. It offers profound insight to family members, friends, lovers, and counselors who, in the name of protecting themselves or others, may have inadvertently harmed victims on their road to survivorship.

Dear Sister is divided into six chapters featuring traditional-style letters, poetry, essays, and interviews. Each entry is an invaluable resource taking the reader on a journey where healing and survivorship are central, and shame, blame, and stigma don't even touch the margins. While there are similarities and even some parallel journeys, no entry is the same. This isn't a one-size-fits-all compilation because the road to healing from sexual violence isn't monolithic. Instead, eloquent and extremely diverse testimonials are preserved as distinct voices in one anthology. Lisa Factora-Borchers' editorial eye found the threads that connect each entry to the other, which are breaking silences through unconditional love. For, as Black Feminist Lesbian Mother Warrior Poet Audre Lorde said, "It is not differences, that immobilize us, but silence."

Each offering could be excerpted, but I will only highlight a few excerpts from each chapter with the affirmation that you, Dear Reader, will gift yourself the incredible internal and external expedition that this anthology has to offer everyone…

What Every Survivors Needs to Know:
- "Loving yourself is one of the important things you can do for your peace of mind."

- "It wasn't your fault; it was never your fault. You did nothing wrong. Hold this tight to your heart; it wasn't your fault."

- "I believe you."

- "Moving forward is not a choice. It is a requirement."

A Child Re-members:
- "I am 49 years old, I remember…"

- "I am writing to you, Dear Sister, to tell you I am out here. That we are out here, all of us. We are the walking wounded who lived through it and are often confused and lonely. Yes, just like you."

Family Ties:
- "I think it's important for you to know that I am sixty-five years old and have carried this 'secret' since I was seven years old."

- "I can't leave the brothers out, not just

because some of them are our sisters, too, but because some of them were our sisters, and are now our brothers, building masculinity into something we can live with, celebrate, challenge, and transform."

- "It is not my fault.
  It would've still happened if I were smarter, tougher, angrier, nicer…
  It's not my fault.
  It's not your fault either.
  Nothing you could've done could've changed what happened."

- "Your actions are your own and do not reflect the unjust and violent actions that were forced upon you."

- "I have hope that together we can figure out a better way to deal with the violence that is woven into every layer of our individual and collective lives. And most of all, I hope that you, too, find your healing path."

From Trauma to Strength:

- "You must decide what is justice for you. Just know that you are not crazy. You are believed. And you deserve justice."

- "I did not come to this work, the work of transformative and disability justice, to be healed. I came to transformative justice because it was the only framework I found that could hold the complexities of intimate and state violence, accountability and healing, and systemic and personal transformation…. I am not a healer, but I am an organizer, a community builder, and an evidence-leaver for those coming after me. As a survivor of violence, I do not wish violence on anyone, even those who have perpetrated violence. Nor do I wish more trauma, terror, or shame to those who have caused trauma, terror, or shame. I know that this is not the way to liberation—I feel it in my bones, my spirit, and my soul."

- "I do not hurt myself, or act in ways that contribute to my self-destruction, the self-destruction the world wants me to take part in. I also do not act in ways that are destructive to my community, because we are interdependent."

Radical Companionship:

- "Surviving is the process of living and dying each day. A primordial balancing. The ability to walk through level-five earthquakes. When you feel the impossible breathing down your neck, you are on the right path. As long as you continue moving—whether you crawl, wander, or run—your energy will keep you alive."

- "I am angry at the unfairness of my condition. I am a veteran of an unnamed war. I have no home to return to, ravaged by conflict. I escaped with my life. It is not fair. There are so many who do not get out alive."

- "come on sister
  we're almost there

can you feel
my hand in yours?
can you see the star
with its healing light
guiding us back home?"

- "But, Sister, you have millions of warrioresses who are eternally committed to you. We see you. You are greater, stronger, and much more enduring than the evil that has been done to you. You are infinitely valuable. And you are never alone. As you continue your fight to survive and to heal, know that we are fighting with you. We will challenge those who allowed this to happen to you. We will walk with you, listen to you, support you, and offer you our unconditional acceptance. We are here—unwavering—as your comrades, as your defenders, as your sisters."

Choose Your Own Adventure:

- "I can't even begin to express how happy I am to be writing this. To get the chance to actually be a part of this movement for hope? Well, hot damn! Sign me up."

- "Sister, don't be afraid of what happens next. Don't pretend to be happy and don't be silent if that's not who you are. Embrace every feeling, grieve if you need to, rejoice when you want. You aren't wrong for feeling anything that you feel."

- "I sing the song
I am not a victim

I am not a survivor
I am a phoenix rising above my own ashes
I am a warrior
I am a warrior of the Mother line
reclaiming the cunts of her daughters
and my Mothers dance
and my Mothers sing
along with me."

Through this stunning mosaic of words, Sister Lisa Factora-Borchers gives all of us—survivors and allies—a new way to envision compassionate radical change in the world, whose foundation is built upon unconditional love for all survivors, regardless. *Dear Sister* is the gift that will keep on giving to survivor and ally after survivor and ally after survivor and ally after survivor and ally. Each entry leaves its indelible imprint on one's psyche and spirit. *Dear Sister* is a call for unconditional transformative love and justice in our familial, platonic, intimate, professional, activist, and spiritual lives. It challenges all of us to re-envision a healing model that encompasses a diversity of voices that may not agree on the specific path to healing but have unanimity that healing, unconditional self-love, and transformative justice—however we each compassionately define it—is the way out of trauma.

Read it for yourself. Share it widely, because there are more of us in our midst that have been impacted by sexual violence than there are who have not. For those who are on the survivor journey and for the many more who have yet to embark on it, *Dear Sister* is a non-judgmental resource that offers numerous options on this complex path to self-love.

Lisa Factora-Borchers

DEAR SISTER/ QUERIDA HERMANA: INTRODUCTION

Language is the house of being.
—Martin Heidegger—

A woman-of-color who writes poetry or
paints or dances or makes movies knows
there is no escape from race or gender
when she is writing or painting. She
can't take off her color and sex and leave
them at the door of her study or studio.
Nor can she leave behind her history.
Art is about identity, among other
things, and her creativity is political.
—Gloria Anzaldúa—

Beyond Literary Arms

One late night in the fall of 2001, I nearly fainted in a hospital room. In a small town called Aberdeen, tucked away in a foggy county of Grays Harbor in Washington, I was working as a legal and medical advocate for survivors of sexual violence. I remember describing it once as a job built for people with their own oxygen tanks—they needed to breathe more frequently and more deeply than others. I learned my lesson the hard way that night.

A patient had asked for an advocate during her medical exam, which was not an unusual request, and I had a routine for preparing myself before seeing a survivor for the first time after their assault. What survivors need in that moment is wide-ranging, and this particular survivor was difficult to hear. Her speech was flattened and mumbled. At times she was incoherent. Against a wall in a small examining room with a busy doctor and uncomfortable nurse, I had little room to do much for the survivor except meet her eyes when she raised her head and make small nods affirming that I was still with her.

Her pain was excruciatingly audible and the line between advocate and survivor began to blur. The doctor kept telling her to relax and my desire to shout, "How would you suggest she go about that?" would not help the situation. She couldn't breathe, nor could I. Her muffled cries were palpable. The smell of paperwork and dry cotton clung to my nostrils. Her face, the frustrated hands of the doctor, I didn't realize the room had run out of oxygen until I started seeing stars. Before I caused even more chaos, I excused myself so I could gather my wits. I was unraveling.

I scrambled past the police officers waiting outside the examination room to a nearby restroom, sat down, and leaned over my knees to put my head between my legs. The story of this survivor was just beginning, but all the survivors I'd worked with prior to that night were running through my head. Most of the legal battles I worked on were lost, survivors disappearing into the shadows after humiliating and traumatizing processes that rarely led to conviction or anything resembling healing.

As the stars faded, as my vision straightened itself, as I sat in a hospital bathroom, I started wondering how to get my breath back and how to do something useful with it beyond legal advocacy.

Six years later, after working in a variety of contexts addressing sexual violence, I received a jarring e-mail. It came from a friend (and a contributor to this anthology), Alexis Pauline Gumbs. As I read it, the familiar squeeze came and tightened its grip on my lungs. I wasn't passing out, but her message stole my breath again. Someone in her community had just been raped, Alexis explained, and she was asking us to write a letter to this particular woman— to uplift her, surround her in community. I had no idea what to write. I didn't even know her name, but something beckoned me to connect with this survivor. I found my breath again, sat up straight in my chair, and began to type.

As I wrote the letter, I thought of the faces of both survivors and perpetrators in my life; friends, family, clients, and coworkers. I thought of my friends who disclosed stories of being raped by strangers, lovers, spouses, friends, acquaintances, caretakers, and family members. I knew and loved so many survivors. And slowly, I came to the shaky realization that some of those people I loved were also perpetrators.

Three years later, with just a handful of years as an assistant magazine editor and an organic vision, I sent out a call for submissions to survivors and allies, asking each of them to write a letter to a survivor of sexual violence. I called the project *The Dear Sister Anthology*.

I tapped every network and contact I could think of, sending the call out in the academic world via a listserv I gained access to while working at a university women's center. It spread through contacts I had made by blogging, presenting at conferences, and doing feminist activist work. At the time, I was working with the independent feminist magazine *make/shift*, and I included the call in their community bulletin board. Although I had rented a P.O. box and listed the mailing address for those who did not have Internet access, the Internet was largely responsible for *Dear Sister*'s circuit around the world, flying on the wings of communities and groups I had grown to know and trust, who forwarded and shared this grassroots project.

Shortly after the call went out, I received two e-mails expressing their discomfort with the project's focus. The first, a director of an urban YMCA, asked me to be mindful of the word "women." She urged me to include the trans population who may not identify with the word. I thanked her for pointing it out and incorporated her suggestion so the call targeted "women and women-identified survivors and allies." The second person's e-mail spilled over with anger, claiming that I was ignoring the fact that men and boys are raped. The anthology's focus on solely women-identified people, she argued, further alienated men-identified survivors. Her message concluded with insults and derogatory assumptions.

Despite the accusatory tone of this particular missive, I took her underlying message seriously and responded with my reasons for focusing solely on women and women-identified survivors. The project does not seek to disrespect or deny the existence of men and men-identified survivors, I wrote. The call for submissions was not meant to make a definitive statement about the survivor landscape of rape; it was giving parameter to a massive issue. This particular anthology would focus on one particular subset.

These two messages ushered in healthy agitation against the gender binary and, looking back, I understand that my responses sprung from my own experiences and interpretations of feminism, activism, and counseling. It came from my periphery which included primarily survivors who were cisgender women with US citizenship, literacy skills, access to the Internet, with time to reflect, who are able-bodied, English speaking, actively in contact with local coalitions, and identified their perpetrators as men. It was through this lens that I wrote the framework for the anthology. And it was out of this framework that I grew as well.

Beyond Sisterhood

I chose the title "Dear Sister" to evoke intimacy, mimicking the facilitated exchange of that 2007 letter. I used the title to build a bridge. The title came with an invisible assumption that "sister" was our common bond, as if gender alone assured a safe and open space, forgetting that the word carries its own etymology.

Politically, "sister" carries a stormy history, stemming from the second-wave feminists who often used it in blind and condescending erasure of women of color and other marginalized communities. It has been used to demarcate the era of privileged white-presenting feminists who placed their agenda on the backs of marginalized women, in racist, capitalist, and imperialist acts against their "sisters" of color. "Sister" has been used to define and create so-called safe places, using gender as a cornerstone for relationship building. It has been co-opted, appropriated, reclaimed, exalted, and misused in feminist and activist groups.

Inclusivity is marked not just by the language we use, but also by the invisible assumptions we leave in the white spaces between words. Originally, I had hoped that the words "Dear Sister" would coax the reader into a place of kinship with the contributor, but genuine connection cannot be built solely on familiarity or sameness, be it gender, race, sexuality, class, belief, or physical ability.

What binds us all is our found interdependence, knowing that individual trauma can be carried with others in the pursuit of radical freedom from systematic oppression. What will bind you to the contributors is their wisdom, humor, and transformative poetic insights, not the assumption that the writer shares your gender or sexual identity. Once you've passed the membrane of the cover, survivors sing their truths from these pages. And no choir soars on sameness, but rather on harmonies of different chords, tones, and pitches.

We are both inspired and sheltered by our personal experiences and observations of oppression, violence, and healing. My experience of *Dear Sister* transformed my politic. I grew as an activist, more aware of the lives of sex workers, queer and femme survivors, the power of erotic poetry, nuanced possibilities of forgiveness, and the pathless negotiations each survivor must confront on their own.

These realizations about the controversial title, that using "sister" to generate intimacy was a cultural truth for some, not universal truth for all, surfaced late in the process. I had two options: (1) change the title and risk altering the framework that each contributor used to write their piece, or (2) keep the title, metabolize the lesson, and write a deconstructionist perspective of the process in the introduction.

I think it's clear what I chose.

Some of the most enlightening conversations came out of this dilemma. Alexis Pauline Gumbs shared with me over the phone that celebrating queer black feminism has been met with similar challenges over the use of the word "sister." She didn't tell me what to do, she just repeatedly affirmed the project and walked with me in the struggle. Aaminah Shakur chatted with me, offering her initial thoughts that the title sounded like it called for "one to one conversation," while reminding me we cannot predict the impact of the word on any group—cisgender women, women of color, trans women, or genderqueer people—because no group is monolithic and each person will have their own relationship and history with it. Mattilda Bernstein Sycamore broke down her brilliance in her analysis of "sister" and how the word carries a "legacy of the '80s, of second-wave feminism." Sofia Rose Smith reminded me to breathe, to do what I could and balance what I could not.

Each person both challenged and comforted me. There was no threat present in being challenged, just honest reflection of the power of language and the ongoing learning to navigate inclusion.

I chose to keep the title because I didn't want to ignore the evolution of the book or shortchange the story of its completion. I also didn't want to pretend the book was something it was not. Even with the best

intentions, we all hold the peril of excluding and harm
ing others when we work in the real time of writing,
publishing, deadlines, personal evolution, and com-
munication. My hope is that this introduction helps
explain a bit of the title's origin and intention, and the
reader finds value in the unfolding story of the title. I
chose to be transparent about this process and hope
that it enriches the conversation about feminist praxis.
I hope it contributes to the work already being done to
transform language, policies, and systems in the practice of reflection, ongoing community building, liberation, and spiritual resistance training.

Beyond the Systems

Dear Sister speaks a different language. Its language
comes from the survivors whose lives refract the intersecting beams of systematic repression and cultural
norming. Activists, pundits, and media makers often
remark that we need to have a "bigger conversation"
or "change the conversation" on sexual violence. For
that kind of shift to occur in our international, national, and local communities, it is imperative that
the conversations scrutinize the interlocking forces of
the criminal justice system, mainstream media, and
legislative policies that interrogate (at best) the survivors, even if the survivor is a child. If these topics are
absent from any conversation claiming to end sexual
violence, the conversation is redundant.

In these personal narratives, the contributors offer readers a glimpse into the interface of systems
and cultures. While the anthology includes reflec-
tions from survivors who chose to report and utilize

the legal system, it's impossible to ignore the glaring overarching truth: the criminal justice system fails survivors of sexual violence. This is especially true for survivors of color who are women, trans women, gender non-conforming, indigenous, disabled, undocumented, poor, or identify with any disenfranchised community. Not only is the process inaccessible, but it also could potentially endanger the life and/or livelihood of a survivor and their family.

If we are to create alternatives to reporting, prosecution, and incarceration, we must first understand the passive ways in which we all encounter, condone, and consume messages of power, gender essentialism, sexism, and violence. This is a daunting task, but if we are serious about "changing the conversation," this is the task at hand. If communities are to create viable options for survivors and perpetrators seeking to redefine justice and healing, it's important to know that building accountability systems within subcultures is still new territory, but it's growing. As Mia Mingus writes in her essay about disability and transformative justice, we must focus on models that do not impose further harm to either survivor or perpetrator. Transformative justice is premised upon "community-based responses to violence that don't collude with state, communal, or systemic violence." It calls for nuanced anti-violence work that seeks the transformation of both survivor and perpetrator in safe, healing, and long-lasting ways. Transformative work is often the political and personal work that we shy away from because of its inherent ability to destabilize our notions and identities of gender, sexuality, and security.

Removing rapists, perpetrators, and predators from the rest of society feeds a false notion that these individuals were born knowing how to denigrate others, rape, and cause harm. It focuses on "it's THEM not us" as the problem, instead of evaluating one's participation in the culture that creates and sustains sexual violence. Rather than assuming responsibility as cultural workers, most people are indifferent and accept mainstream notions of justice: placing perpetrators behind bars where they are likely to become, if they are not already, survivors of sexual violence. Meanwhile, the same ideologies that taught perpetrators how to groom, silence, harm, threaten, stalk, manipulate, beat, and rape remain unchanged. The cultural overtures that prime our youth and teach them about gender, power, worth, and violence are recycled for a new generation of survivors and perpetrators.

The very basic level of healing and justice begins with the innermost circle of loved ones and community of survivors and perpetrators. Most family members and communities are not aware of, let alone build on this power. True spaces of justice are the spaces where vulnerability is a sign of strength, where choice is honored, and listening is a transformative tool for activism.

Beyond Survival

It is my deepest hope and most fervent prayer that the conversations and challenges that spring from these pages support and challenge you in ways that give you new life. Even if it's not sexual violence, we all have survived something. I built this space for you, for me, for all of us. It was never meant to be a haven away from the world, but rather a safe port to confront it and ourselves.

ACKNOWLEDGEMENTS

This anthology would not be possible without the support of so many people.

I would first like to thank Jessica Hoffman whose visionary work with *make/shift* magazine taught me the love-centered practices of editing as a revolutionary act. Quite simply, I could not have begun this project without your work and the lessons I learned from your practices.

To Alexis Pauline Gumbs: Without your wisdom and grace-filled reminders about the power of letters, this anthology would not have come to fruition. Your tireless radical feminist brilliance has uplifted me more times than I can count.

For her energy, commitment, and spirit, I am indebted to Aishah Shahidah Simmons who not only agreed to write the foreword for this book, but who also collaborated with me to support the project. Both your academic and artistic work to end sexual violence has taught me, and future generations, infinite lessons about creativity and perseverance.

I would not have been able to envision *Dear Sister* had it not been for the people, co-workers, clients, and friends in Aberdeen, Washington. It was in this town that I first learned about working with survivors of incest and sexual assault. For all my clients who shared their lives with me and sought peace in the aftermath of their violation, *Dear Sister* belongs to you.

A very special thanks to Mandy Van Deven for being the first eyes to look over the skeletons of the manuscript and offer friendship and support during some of the hardest parts of editing.

A big thank you to my dear friend Claire Mugavin Pfister for translating "For All That Left Her."

To all the great folks at AK Press for taking on this anthology, especially to Kate Khatib and Christa B. Daring who personally worked with me to finally move the vision into a paged reality: thank you.

I cannot adequately express my love and gratitude to each who wrote a letter, essay, or poem and offered their voice for this project, and most especially to the contributors in this anthology. Thank you for your work, heart, and generosity to share your stories with the world. It has been an honor and privilege to walk with you.

And finally, the most profound thanks goes to the person who sat through the years of ideas, slumps, and epiphanies: my life partner, Nick. Without you, I would not have as much love in my life or enough to give to this work. Thank you for co-parenting and co-creating with me so our son is raised in a non-violent world. Thank you for believing in this project, in its completion, and in my ability to see it through.

Editor's Note on "Triggering"

Many online pieces of literature have used a "trigger warning" as a precursor to materials that may shift the reader's emotional or psychological state to an unsafe or unstable place. This may be particularly true for survivors who may be susceptible to a variety of reactions because of rhetoric and imagery when discussing violence, abuse, and sexual trauma.

Each contributor I worked with was encouraged to practice radical self-care as we went through numerous stages of editing their work. Writing involves remembering perhaps the darkest or most unresolved part of someone's life. Each piece reflects a part of the personality and memory of its contributor, and though they are threaded by a common denominator of compassion, no two are alike. What may have been healing for the contributor to use—images and words centering on body, consent, sexual expression, justice, and suffering—may have a different impact on the reader.

Be gentle with yourself and practice self-care as you absorb these works. Only you can know when to put the book down to rest or when to pick it up again to walk with another contributor.

Be care-full. Be brave. You are not alone.

What Every Survivor
Needs to Know

Ana Heaton

THE SECRET OF ME

I am:
 A bookshelf on a latch
   A concealed stairway to hide secrets and
homemade preserves
      A lopsided yellow flower thriving
         between the cracks of ill used sidewalks
         nowhere to go but up

An Ally

LETTER 1: KEEP BREATHING

Dear Sister,

Keep breathing.

You may have to measure time in breaths for a while. You will have a minute, and then an hour, and then a day when it isn't so hard to let your chest rise and fall. When you don't feel the weight of so much pain. You will have a day.

One day, without you even realizing what happened, the weight will be lifted for a moment. You will be happy. Something beautiful will catch your eye, or something will make you laugh.

For now, you are here. Maybe you feel you are broken. Maybe you are broken. Maybe the whole world is broken. But there is something that is not broken. You can find it.

Look for it one breath at a time.

Love,
An Ally

Birdy

LETTER 2: WHAT I SHOULD HAVE BEEN TOLD

Dear Sister,

These are the things I wish I had been told:

I love you. I love you.

Loving yourself is the best way to defeat your attacker. Say *I love you* to yourself every day. On the days you can't say it, use one of the *I love you*s from above. Loving yourself is one of the important things you can do for your peace of mind.

You are loved. You are loved.

Always remember that there are people that love you. They may be in your life, they may no longer be in your life. You may not even know them, but their hands are for you to hold, their shoulders are for you to cry on, and their love will be there any time you need.

Love always,
Your sister

Aaminah Shakur

LETTER 3: IT WASN'T YOUR FAULT

Dear Sister,

It wasn't your fault; it was never your fault. You did nothing wrong. Hold this tight to your heart: it wasn't your fault.

At night when you lay there and your mind fills with images and you wonder *if only, if you had...if you hadn't*...remember, it wasn't your fault.

When you talk to someone—family, friend, therapist, co-worker, another survivor—you will get the sense that they wonder why you wore that, went there, didn't think, didn't know, seemed willing, were unsure and unclear, didn't scream, didn't bite...*why why why*...remember, no matter what they tell you, it wasn't your fault.

If you whispered, "I love you," it still wasn't your fault.

If you let it be known that you like girls instead, it still wasn't your fault.

If you had said yes before, it did not give permission this time, and it still wasn't your fault.

If you said "maybe later," it still wasn't your fault that he wouldn't wait.

If you slept with his friend or "everyone knows

you're easy," it doesn't mean they own you and have a right. It still wasn't your fault.

If you let him in when he was drunk in the middle of the night, it was not an invitation to sex, and it still wasn't your fault.

You didn't confuse him. You did not owe him for anything. You didn't deserve it.

You didn't make him do it, drive him crazy, make it easier, give him unspoken permission.

When he ignored your words, when he touched you without your permission, when he used your body against your wishes—it was his fault. Not yours.

It was never your fault. Hold this tight to your heart.

LETTER 4: YOUR LIGHT

Dear Sister,

There was a hole inside of me.

For days, weeks, months, I couldn't stand it: the pain, the questioning, the wondering, the surges of mixed feelings coursing through my body. He'd hurt me, violated me, torn me apart with his words, his touch, and his apathy. Curling into a small ball, I hoped to minimize my presence in this world, to become smaller and smaller, until, eventually, I could completely disappear.

I was broken.

And then I was saved. Not by God, or any goddess. Not by any higher power. I was saved by my self, by the light deep down inside me. One day, from the depths of the darkness inside of me, there was a spark of light. This spark refused to be put out, regardless of how hard I tried. This light sustained me; it saved me.

This light is in you, and it *is* you. It is the happier moments in your life; it is your spark, your spirit, and your strength. As you tend to it, this light will grow, giving you whatever it is that you need to survive.

This light is the strength you need to reclaim your life. It is the power to re-enter the world as a strong(er), powerful woman. It is what you need to leave your partner, to file a complaint with the police or courts, to move away, to go back to that park/ room/store/bar, or to never go back again. Whatever it is *you* need to do, that is exactly what the light will help you to do.

I know you have this light and once you find it, it grows. As people around you continue to support you, it grows even more. Your own hopes, dreams, and even letting go of your fears will also feed this luminary source. It will expand its glow from deep inside your heart and help you shine in this world of ours.

Perhaps it is a tiny flicker, or just a muted glow, but it's there, I promise. You and you alone have enough strength to survive. Friends, family, and others can help, but you already have it inside. Just allow yourself to find that light, to embrace its power, to let it show you the way.

Just when it seems like the dark will swallow you whole, that is when you must find your light. Reach out to it, and then reach out to others.

You are not alone. You are never alone.

Shanna

LETTER 5: I BELIEVE YOU

Dear Sister,

I believe you.

I knew the man who attacked me. We had dated exclusively at one point and I had even considered him a close friend. The day after it happened, he called me to tell me he wanted to come over to my apartment to "talk about it."

I told him no.

He came over anyway.

I stood in the kitchen washing dishes while he sat to my left at the table, trying to get me to look at him, to acknowledge his words, to sit down and talk with him "like a reasonable adult."

The table was white. My roommate and I barely used the table at all except as a place to leave our stuff when we came in the door. But at that moment, it was empty except for him sitting there, anxiously trying to make me sit down for a "real talk."

"Come on," he said after I refused to sit down, "you're being completely unreasonable about this."

I didn't have the cutting remarks on my tongue just yet. It was too fresh. I just said, "I'm not being unreasonable. I want you to leave."

"You know I can't leave until we both understand what happened. I don't know why you're acting this way."

I was incredulous at the same time that I was heartbroken. I stood there, elbow-deep in soapy water, unable to do anything except wash dishes.

This was the man whom I had loved my freshman year. And this was the same guy who, the night before, had asked me in that same voice, "But we've done it before; why is this time any different? I thought you liked it rough."

I had never been afraid of his weight or strength before; I'd never been given a reason to fear him. He'd been stumbling drunk the previous night and I had even thought to myself, "At least he's not an aggressive drunk." I trusted him.

I had been warned about strangers. I was told to always walk in groups and to keep a buddy with me at all times. I never thought that he, who had always been protective of me in the past, would end up being the very person I needed to be protected from.

I was in denial. It couldn't have been…that. The word "rape" was too much. I replayed that night in my head again and again as I tried to figure out how I could've prevented it, all the while trying to convince myself that I was overreacting.

He was also trying to persuade me that I was mistaken, and I was furious at him for it; why did he think he knew my own thoughts and feelings better than I did? Here he was, pleading for "a chance to be heard." Here he was, again, not even twenty-four hours later, still unwanted, still forcing himself on me. He had no memory of the previous night, he said, but that I must have misunderstood the situation because he wasn't that kind of guy. He told me I was exaggerating and overreacting and obviously too emotional to really know what I was accusing him of and…

…and I wanted to scream.

I wanted to hurt him the way he'd hurt me. I wanted him to understand. I wanted him to remember. But there, in that moment, elbow-deep in dishwater, none of those things happened.

He said his piece. He even insisted I sit down across from him because he said I wasn't taking the conversation seriously while I was doing other things. He sat there and took what he wanted from me. Again.

Later, after he'd finally left, I called my then-boyfriend and told him—between sobs—what had happened. He said, "Is that all? That doesn't sound so bad; it could've been a lot worse. Are you sure you're not taking this too personally? You might be blowing this out of proportion, don't you think?"

I didn't know what to say. I didn't want to believe it was that bad, either.

But it was.

Sister, I'm not telling you this to gain sympathy or tell you, "I know what it feels like." I'm telling you because I wanted—needed—to be believed but wasn't.

I believe you. And I believe it was as bad as you say it was. I don't know what happened to you, but I believe you.

Viannah

Renée Martin

LETTER 6: PUTTING IT BESIDE YOU

Dear Sister,

I remember like it was yesterday, the day you called and told me that you had been raped. My mind flashed back to one of the most painful days of my life, and I felt my body tighten, as I once again felt his hands around my throat. I didn't hear your pain, because I was drowning in my own. When you reached to me for comfort, I turned to the familiar, well-phrased comment—*it wasn't your fault*—but what I didn't tell you is that even after you accept the truth of those words, you will still have to find a way to live with what he did to you.

There will be many things you will have to face as a survivor. In all of the mixed responses I received after my assault, no one told me what to expect, and so despite the pain that it causes me to relive those dark days, I shall share with you the aftermath of the day that changed my life forever.

You will be questioned about the decisions you made leading up to the rape. Family and friends will advise you to be more careful next time: dress more conservatively, don't drink, don't go out after dark, don't talk to strangers, don't trust people.

Don't, don't, don't.

Some will want you to talk about it incessantly in the mistaken belief that letting it spew from you like an erupting volcano will purge the pain. If you don't cry or tear at your clothes frantically, screaming of a rage born of your violation, they will conclude that you are in denial. Some will want you to remain silent because it allows them to pretend that you are unchanged by the violence, that the world is safe for women.

None of these messages teach you how to live again, and living is what you need to feel whole. This kind of rhetoric exists to make you feel somehow responsible for what is the worst violation someone could ever face. Each person you encounter will expect an emotional performance based in their belief of how a rape survivor behaves and feels. But unless they have been through it, they can't possibly understand where you are coming from.

Dancing like a marionette to please others is the last thing that you will want to do after your body was violated. And when you try to find a way to deal with the rape on your own terms, someone will step forward to correct your decision, once again reminding you that your body is not your own. This feels like another violation, one that stings so sharply that your body burns with rage, but there is no outlet. So you swallow the hurt and the rage, perhaps thinking, *If I just do what everyone says, be who they want me to be—I can sleep at night. Maybe I won't feel his breath on my face or feel like peeling a layer off my skin every time I shower in a desperate bid to rid my body from the feel of his touch.*

Platitudes, fake smiles, and performance don't help you because despite what everyone thinks, rape is not something you can ever put behind you. You cannot fake your way into believing that this did not happen, that everything is "okay." The numbness sets in and rather than dealing with the rage and the pain, you think that it is better not to feel anything at all.

And just like the calm before the storm, when you least expect it, you will be triggered. Perhaps it will be a song, or the sound of footsteps on the pavement, but whatever it is, it will transport you right back to the violation of his touch and you will once again relive the searing pain that burns incandescently, bright and fresh and raw—as if not a single day has passed since everything you held dear was taken from you.

What you need to know, and what no one will be willing to say, is that it is okay to stop trying to put this behind you. It is okay to cry. It is okay to scream, even if these emotions leave you feeling impotent and vulnerable. If ever there was a time in life to be selfish, this is it.

Time will pass and one day you will wake up and realize that you have put this beside you and not behind you. It will travel down every road you go and it will dance with you in the shadows.

Sometimes it will rear its ugly head in your nightmares but you will be able to breathe, feel, and think again as you work through the terrible violation that occurred. The dreams may never totally leave you, but as you find your own voice and learn to center yourself again, they will occur less and you will be able to focus on the here and now. Nothing will ever be the same and that is okay because, in the end, knowing

you have the right to choose and then deciding how
you are going to survive rape will give you back the
autonomy that you thought you had lost.

Renée Martin

Zöe Flowers

CHOOSING LIBERATION AFTER PHYSICAL AND SEXUAL ABUSE: AN INTERVIEW

Zöe, you authored the book Dirty Laundry: Women of Color Speak Up about Dating and Domestic Violence, *which profiles the lives of African-American women who survived intimate partner violence and sexual violence. Can you speak more about the options that survivors, particularly incest survivors, have when seeking healing and justice when they do not have access to or do not choose traditional modalities (e.g. the judicial system or Westernized concepts of emotive therapies)?*

Why don't I tell you what I did that was beyond the scope of traditional services? It never occurred to me to go to a shelter or the police when I ended the relationship with my ex. I didn't realize how much danger I was in until I ran into him one night several months after the break up. I didn't know that one third of women are killed during separation but I instinctively knew that he had turned a dangerous corner that night. He soon began stalking me and threatened to kill himself and me. It was then that I involved the police. They were no help. It was the early '90s and stalking wasn't taken seriously.

Once I knew the police were not an option (even after he broke into my apartment), I immediately began safety planning. All of my planning came from a very intuitive place. I did not listen to friends and family who thought I was exaggerating the level of danger. I did what I felt was best. I moved out of my apartment and in with a friend that he did not know. My employer and I came up with an alias; the security guard was given my partner's picture and my employer allowed me to alter my work schedule. A few months later I left the state. I realize this is not an option for everyone, but for me it was the best thing I could have done.

My healing started when I left home. I began accessing the written word, service to others, creativity, and the world of spirit. I was introduced to the works of Wayne Dyer a few years prior to leaving home, and he was the first person who spoke of how our thoughts impact our reality. This was a concept that I was completely unfamiliar with but it resonated as truth. Then I moved on to books by Iyanla Vanzant. She looked liked me and shared similar experiences. After reading all her books, I began opening up about what had happened to me. I began hosting and attending sister circles and poetry readings. This opened me up to a new group of people that supported me and for the first time my true self started to emerge. This was extremely healing because my creativity was beginning to flourish in new ways. I decided to chronicle other women's stories abuse. And that's how *Dirty Laundry* was born.

The next phase of my healing came from allowing myself to be of service. I started volunteering at a home for AIDS patients, I fed the homeless on Thanksgiving, and I did all sorts of clothing drives, started recycling initiatives at my places of employment, and became a vegetarian. Living this way helped to get out of my own story and to help others! And all along the way, I was diving deeper into the spirit world. I began centering myself through yoga, meditation, learning about metaphysics, and attending a nondenominational church. After years of internal work I began working in the domestic violence movement.

I said all that to say that I never looked to the mainstream to help me. It wasn't even a thought. I think healing, like happiness, is a choice and there are several roads to getting there. My path is through knowing that I cannot only heal myself but that I am creating better experiences every day.

Based on your book Dirty Laundry, *you created a choreo-drama,* From Ashes to Angel's Dust: A Journey Through Womanhood. *Its dedication reads that it is for "our ancestors that died so that we might live—that starved so we might prosper. It is for those silenced by violence, oppression, homophobia, shame or the impulse to please. For all who understand that loving another and oneself is a revolutionary act—the most revolutionary act." What can survivors, who are struggling in the most revolutionary act of loving oneself, do to help prioritize or regain their own sense of self-worth?*

There are so many ways to answer that question. Loving ourselves is full-time job. And it is a hard job because everything in society tells us we are not good enough. However, I believe it the most important job we will ever have. I mean, we have to do it! A crucial factor of loving self is engaging with life and staying in the body. Many of us disassociate from our bodies in one way or another. I had a period of numbing out with food and caffeine. Over the years I have taken drumming lessons, belly dancing, swimming lessons, etc. Anything to keep me in my body.

I also suggest that survivors (or anyone—we're all surviving something) find something that brings them joy and that they are passionate about and do that thing! When I joined the movement a little over ten years ago, I read everything I could on domestic violence. My life was consumed by ending domestic violence. Passion and hard work is often rewarded, and I've been able to speak nationally/internationally and have collaborated with some of the smartest women and men working on this issue. I have a track record now—a template. The impact on my confidence and my ability to believe in myself has been immeasurable.

Track your success not your shortcomings. We all fall short but the creator doesn't make mistakes. If you are here, there is a reason. If you're in the midst of a violent relationship, you can celebrate the fact that you are alive! That means you are resilient, have coping and safety-planning skills. If you're reading this book that means something in you wants a change. Focus on what you are doing to move yourself forward.

You have extensive experience in training professionals and advocates in serving survivors of violence. What are some basic skills and strategies for allies, friends, and family members who are walking with a survivor during their healing process? What are some tools they can practice to avoid secondary emotional trauma and maintain a healthy relationship with a survivor?

I would suggest that friends and family gain a basic understanding of domestic violence and its dynamics. I would suggest advocates need to take this three steps further. I would suggest that advocates become well versed in the herstory of the battered women's and feminist's movement.

One thing that folks need to recognize is that survivors are extremely adept at picking up on nonverbal cues. Their lives are often saved because they have the ability to gage a batterer's behavior and adjust accordingly. What does this mean to you as an advocate or family member? They know if you're judging them. They can feel the "crooked eye" beneath your smile. Not being beaten doesn't make you better or smarter. Be humble. Recognize we all have issues to overcome. Talk less. Listen more. Check your privilege at the door. You are there to support and provide resources. You can't save anyone. You cannot "empower" anyone. Give yourself permission to remove yourself if you must. Be nice. Realize that she is the expert in her situation.

A daily practice of meditation, prayer, yoga, or some other healing modality can help maintain a healthy state of mind. Journaling about your own feelings can be helpful in mitigating some of the effects of vicarious trauma. *Trauma Stewardship* by Laura van Dernoot Lipsky talks about secondary trauma in meaningful way. The book uses humor and van Dernoot Lipksy's razor sharp insight to point out the pitfalls of working in the social services field and provides readers with useful strategies for staying centered.

In your consulting, you offer a workshop for service providers entitled "Sankofa," which is an Akan word that means "We must go back and reclaim our past so we can move forward, in order to enable us to understand why and how we came to be who we are today." Can you elaborate more on "Sankofa" as it pertains to survivors of violence and trauma who struggle with moving forward?

When you realize that people of color (and women) have been "free" for a shorter period of time than we were oppressed, our current state begins to make sense. We have a habit of ignoring history and pretending it has no impact. It was not too long ago that people of color (and women) were thought of as property. That is real. And it is an important fact to understand when talking about violence against women. We need to know our history. We need to know what they tapped into to be able to survive as they did. We must take in the knowledge of who we are as people of color and as women.

We have a shared history of oppression and resilience that must be recognized and resurrected. We are descended from people that survived being packed on ships in configurations that their captives would not put animals in because the animals would perish. And we survived. We lived through 400-plus years of being bought and sold. Four hundred years. That's a long damn time! What it must have been like to have generation after generation born into slavery. How heartwrenching it must have been to be owned by people. And we survived. We are here despite the odds.

Moving forward is not a choice. It is a requirement. I don't believe that my ancestors survived all they did so that some man (or woman) could abuse me and tell me what to do. Each decision we make either keeps us enslaved or liberates us. I choose liberation.

Marianne Kirby

YOU DON'T OWE IT TO ANYONE ELSE TO REPORT

This article was first published in xoJane
and is reprinted with permission.

Sexual assault—of any sort—has intense and personal ramifications for every individual. I don't just mean emotionally. But there are many reasons why someone might not want to report being raped—and they should never be erased.

People who report rape—especially women who belong to vulnerable populations (women of color, poor women, disabled women, trans women, very young women—not to mention people who live at the intersections of these identities)—are scrutinized in our courts and in our popular media. To report a rape can mean being further victimized not just by the victim-blaming system but also by the support structures we thought we had in place, like friends and family and school social circles. It can mean losing a job along with a reputation. It can mean being called a liar, and it can mean being accused of ruining young men's lives.

Beyond that, only 3 percent of rapists ever spend a day in jail. If your rapist is someone known to you (and it's likely that they are), reporting can actively endanger your life. Even if your rapist is not known to you, reporting means making yourself vulnerable in a way that many people cannot handle after an already life-changing violation, especially when there is so little hope of justice. You only have to do a search for "rape" on xoJane.com to see reports of how that all-too-often works out. And if you are serving in the armed forces, odds are high that your rapist is friends with the person you'd report it to—or that the person you'd report it to is your rapist.

Rape is the responsibility of the rapist—no matter what any given person was wearing, no matter how drunk that person might be, no matter what party that person might be at. The person who was raped does not bear the responsibility for preventing their own rape. Similarly, people who have been sexually assaulted are not somehow responsible for preventing their assailant from assaulting other people.

This is, I am sure, going to stand in conflict with how a lot of people feel about basic human decency. And, all other things being equal, yeah, I come down on the side of preventing harm to others in whatever way I can. Which is why, also because of basic human decency, I will not advocate for heaping even more *should*s on the shoulders of those who have been sexually assaulted.

To be as blunt as possible, people who have been sexually assaulted do not owe other people shit. Their only responsibility is to take care of themselves in the best way that they are able. Hopefully, they have actually supportive people around to help take care of them. Hopefully, they have the resources, whatever those resources might be, available to feel safe again. But my hope does not override my realism; many people do not have those resources. And when folks insist that rape must be reported to prevent rapists from preying on other people, it increases the already unreasonable burden on those who may be struggling.

Our system is bullshit. Guilting people into subjecting themselves to it in the hopes that the system will change sacrifices the well-being of the very people who have already been failed by our rape culture. It's not like this is done maliciously. Everyone is scrambling for something to do in the face of an awful thing, I get that. But pressuring victims is not a compassionate course of action.

In some ways, it feels like a catch-22—if we don't report sexual assault, no one realizes how extensive the problem is and nothing changes; if we do report sexual assault, we are disbelieved and mocked and shamed and interrogated and blamed. And nothing changes. I don't know what the solution is. But I don't think it rests in making serial predation feel like our own fault.

Here it is as plain as I can say it: If you have been raped, you do not have any obligation to any other woman to report your rape. It is not your fault you were raped. It is not your fault if the person who raped you rapes other people. That, too, is the fault of the rapist. If you choose to report after a sexual assault, I support you. That is a brave and meaningful action. But if you choose not to report? I am also here to support you. You are not failing other women. Your only responsibility is to take care of yourself. Because the last thing the victim of a sexual assault needs is a damn guilt trip.

A Child Re-members

MEMORY 1999

MAY 13, 1999

I am 49 years old
I remember
I remember
I remember
I remember
I remember
I remember
I remember
I remember
I remember
I remember
I remember

I remember

I remember

I remember

I

Remember

It

I woke up a couple of months ago from an
anxious insomnia's sleep. Wide-awake in the dark.
Steely cold. Hyper alert. Hair standing up on
the back of my neck. Eyes exploding, open and
searching around the room in silent realization.
Feeling the memory rather than seeing it. How
could I have seen it? I was a child in a dark room.
The feeling of a coarse unshaved beard against
my thighs and rubbing between my legs. Scratchy.
The large strong hand holding my ankles apart. The
hands are so big they almost reach to my knees. I
was so little. Feeling pinned. I remember. I remember.
I know. I know. I know. It was my father. It was my
father. It was my father. It was my father.

   IT WAS MY FATHER
   IT WAS MY FATHER
   IT WAS MY FATHER
   IT WAS MY FATHER
   IT WAS MY FATHER

I lay awake the rest of the night figuring it out.
Putting it all together. The childhood dreams of
someone chasing me. A nightmare. Night terrors. The
nightmare of a man in a car chasing me. Running
running running running. Panting panting panting,
hurting hurting hurting. The car catches up to me. I

turn. The man gets out of the car. It is my father. The dream repeats repeats repeats repeats repeats repeats repeats for years and years and years and years.

IT WAS MY FATHER
IT WAS MY FATHER
IT WAS MY FATHER
IT WAS MY FATHER
IT WAS MY FATHER

Night terrors. I can't sleep in the dark. I need to have a light on. "Judy is afraid of the dark." My brother and mother make fun of me. I am terrified of darkness. I scream and cry when my mother tries to make me turn off the light. I wake up terrified. I hear snoring in my room on the other side of the bed. It is loud. It is snoring like my father. My father snores just like that. Snoring terrifies me. Snoring is a night terror.

IT WAS MY FATHER
IT WAS MY FATHER
IT WAS MY FATHER
IT WAS MY FATHER
IT WAS MY FATHER

I wet the bed. Why did that happen? I wet the bed every night. When did that start? I was too big. I had already had a dry bed for years. The doctor says there is nothing wrong with me that a good spanking won't fix. He holds up his large man's hand like a paddle when he tells this to my mother. I am still lying on the exam table exposed. My little girl's body. Man terrors. Night terrors.

IT WAS MY FATHER
IT WAS MY FATHER
IT WAS MY FATHER
IT WAS MY FATHER
IT WAS MY FATHER

IT

WAS

MY

FATHER

where was my mother
she knew

Sarah Cash

I'M THERE AGAIN

Preening bottles of perfume, lined up on shelves, their necks turned like pageant queens, and we're sifting through scents, turning smells like pages in books. I shake my head or nod, uncommitted to that, or arrogant to this. Then I smell something powdery and youthful that I would've spritzed on a cloud of as a child, and it's so fucking hard.

I'm there again.

I am playing on the floor with multi-colored plastic ponies spread around me, braiding their manes. He enters the room silently, and I feel him pressing into my back, hot breath in my ear. I dread these moments as they unfold, my childhood being stolen from me. All of my life's firsts would be ruined by those doors he kept closed with my baby dolls' crib scooted in front. His melting blue face in the TV glare worse than shark bites at sea.

The soft innocent scent of girlhood mingling with the hot damp smell of sex, man, and fear as he manipulates my body and mouth to do things I don't understand but inherently know are wrong.

I'm there!

Straight-backed little girl with knocking knees and a silent mouth, and under my red school uniform, I'm screaming as another explores.

Another memory wafts up: I'm in the bathroom with the bad girls, smoking and talking about blow-jobs. I want to punch one of the girls in the face when she ridicules another girl, a "naïve one" for not knowing the term "blow job." But oh, my silent mouth that doesn't defend her because they might guess my past. A cowardly stone in my stomach.

I remember the sting of the wire end of the fly swat on the back of my legs when a relative had finally caught us in the act. I thought I'd been saved, but no. I imagined jumping off mountains, ripping briars through my hand—anything to avoid remembering what had repeatedly happened and the guilt I then bore from the accusations of those who loved me.

I look into the sink's stainless steel bottom, staring at my fuzzy reflection. Silent, being punished for a crime I never committed. My victimization was swallowed with shame. I wore my guilt laced through my hair, dirty unraveled ribbons.

Above the many memories of that time that arose frequently later in my life, I polished hate into smooth little stones. I know every bone, hair, and scratch on myself. I know every single story I've told. I know how it feels to burn yourself alive, to be dead for so many years.

And because of what happened then and how it changed me forever, I now love. I love the flawed. I love the paunch of my stomach, the wrinkles around his eyes, and the beauty of her dragging her crippled leg behind her. I love their lazy eyes, and I love their mushed brains. I love scars; I love the bruises.

I love those shattered, with the hollow in the bend of their arm that holds a cupful of secrets that you'll probably never know.

Because really, all these broken,
 all these survivors.

Mary Zelinka

LETTER 7: THE SPIRAL

Dear Sister,

I have before me a snapshot of myself on Dark Destiny. It's a small, thin, black and white photo, the kind that drugstores used to develop. I'm twelve. Even though the image is blurry, the expression on my face is clear: this horse, this life, is all I have ever dreamed of, ever wanted. A few weeks after this picture is taken I would ride in my first horseshow.

Days later, my trainer will begin molesting me.

When I tell you it isn't your fault, that there is nothing you could have done in your wildest darkest moment to deserve what happened to you, I am also saying it to this twelve-year-old girl on her horse. And to my seventeen-year-old self, my eighteen, nineteen, twenty—all the selves who lived through increasingly violent relationships until at last my thirty-year-old self woke up one morning and said, "I want something different. I don't know what, I just want it to be different."

It would be a lie to say I know what you are going through. All I really know is my own story. My experience in working through my own healing and hearing many other survivors' stories tells me that while there are many similarities, no two of us are alike. Like some kind of wounded snowflakes.

Still, I wish I could tell you the path to follow, give you a roadmap to make your journey easier. But then it would be my map, and that map didn't even work for me all the time. And it would presume that I know what you need better than you do.

What I can say without ever even laying eyes on you is that you are a courageous, strong, and creative person who did not deserve to be sexually abused. How can I be so sure about that? Because you survived. It takes an enormous amount of courage to survive sexual abuse, and you did that. And rather than stuffing the pain, you have chosen to reach out by reading this book. What a gift to yourself! Now you have to trust that the courage and creativity that allowed you to survive can sustain you through your healing.

My own healing journey has lasted for years. I wasted too much time believing the abuse was my fault. I think in some way I actually wanted it to be my fault, because if it were, then I could have control over whether it happened again. But in truth, there is nothing I could have done, just like there is nothing you could have done. Someone *chose* to hurt us. It wasn't my fault, and it wasn't your fault.

Someone chose to hurt you, and the "normal" you knew before is gone forever. The trick now is to create a new normal. By the time I turned thirty, I had thought my life was over—that I would never again experience happiness or joy; that the most I could ever hope for was some kind of bland half-life. I trudged through my days as though I were in quicksand until suicide seemed to be the next logical step. But after a few failed attempts, I decided I might just as well hang around and see what was going to happen next. That was over thirty years ago. Now, not one day goes by that I am not immeasurably grateful that I am still alive.

Sometimes I think survivors who have done their healing work live their lives more deeply than other people. There's a loss in that; we can never take our safety—emotional or physical—for granted again. But there's a gift in that loss. (Not a gift like "I'm so happy this bad thing happened to me because now I'm a stronger person," because basically, that's bullshit. We don't need to have bad things happen to us in order to be strong.) The gift is that we know how precious each peaceful moment really is. We can't go through life on autopilot. Our eyes are open.

My own healing process has been like an outwardly reaching spiral. Picture a cowboy twirling a lariat: At first the spiral was so tight that I couldn't take a deep breath. The sexual assaults stained every waking moment. Then, gradually, the spiral became wider, and when I thought about the violence, it had less hold on me. The spiral has continued to spread wider and wider. The memory of the abuse and its impact will never be forgotten, but it no longer dictates who I am.

What I believe is this: If you keep putting one foot in front of the other and doing your healing work, you will get to the other side. You have to hang on with your fingernails when the pain threatens to overtake you. You have to trust that it won't last forever.

The journey is worth it.

That twelve-year-old girl on her horse was alone all those years ago, but she isn't anymore. Now she has me.

In sisterhood,
Mary Zelinka

LETTER 8: I AM

Dear Sister,

I am nine years old. I am lying on the floor of the kitchen in my own home. There is the clock on the wall that ran out of time long ago and nobody has ever wound it up again. There on the table is the biscuit I was eating a few minutes ago. The margarine is leaking bright yellow from one side and I can still taste the home-canned strawberry jam, made by my mama's hands. The man on top of me is grunting and moaning. My belly hurts. I want my mama but she is at the store buying things for the birthday party for the man who suddenly turned into a monster. The monster looks almost like my step daddy but can't be because he is hurting me and my step daddy is nice to me. I don't understand and I am...

I am sixteen years old and staring up at the roof of the car, seeing a slice of the night sky over the sweaty shoulder of the boy who says he loves me, and wondering why do so many guys love me but always leave? I don't understand and I am...

I am twenty years old and in the hospital bed feeling the final slippery rush as my daughter finally leaves my body to claim a place of her own in this world. I am looking down at her and thinking if anything happens to her I will never forgive myself. I am...

I am twenty-three years old and cooking in a kitchen while the guy I am supposed to be in love with but cannot feel any connection to is in my living room with his friend watching a game, and the only thing I can think is that I have to make him leave because I have a girl child and I don't like him being around her because anything can happen. I wonder why it is that sometimes I feel nothing at all and if I am...

I am twenty-five years old and tracing the shape of my lover's face with trembling hands and wondering if I am really gay or just afraid of men. If I am...

I am thirty years old and trying to talk to my mother about the past without laying the blame and I cannot explain my shame and the total disconnect I sometimes feel. I cannot tell her that what I really need is for someone to apologize to me. I am in need of an apology. I am...

I am thirty-six years old and watching the sky for rain. The man next to me at the football game nudges his friend and I watch them watch the teenage cheerleaders do their flips, and I see the way their eyes go greedy and narrow and I shove a foot into one's ribs and growl out, "Hey perv, that's my kid," and I somehow feel violated. I don't know why but I am...

I am forty-one years old and my daughter is grown and strong. I am a survivor but of what I am not sure. I am a veteran of a war that has many faces and names but always ends with the wounded feeling all the pain, and I spend most of my days wondering if there is any such thing as justice. I am…

I am writing to you, Dear Sister, to tell you I am out here. That we are out here, all of us. We are the walking wounded who lived through it and are often confused and lonely. Yes, just like you. Dear Sister, how are you feeling today? Have you found a way to get out of bed and not think about being the girl whose heart was broken under her daddy's weight and the realization that there was no shelter in the ones we were supposed to be able to trust?

Dear Sister, I love you and hope you are okay.

Best,
Your sister, Angel

LETTER 9: AGAINST ALL ODDS

Dear Sister,

It seems like there aren't many of us out there. I know of only two others, one of them was my sister who took her own life. I believe, though, that there has to be more of us out there. There must be more of us who survived being forced into a sex ring or child prostitution. I know we are not alone. We can't possibly be alone.

But, if nothing else—there is you and me.

Thinking I was alone sometimes felt like the hardest part. Though I have friends who were molested or raped, I don't believe they really know what it is like to be bought and sold like a fast food meal. Their pain and violation is as real as ours, but knowing there is a price on your sex, your vulnerability, and sense of self is something that so few of us can understand.

I understand.

You are not alone. We are not alone.

I know what it is like to be standing there waiting for the finalization of the arrangement and all you can think about is how to not feel the pain and still stay present enough to make yourself believe you have made the assault shorter, or at least you haven't made it any longer. I know what it is like to lie there, a bleeding broken girl, and watch a payment for you pass over. I know that refusing or resisting doesn't just mean punishment from the man in front of you but it also means more brutality waiting from the person who made the sale. Whatever your body was sold for—cash or cocaine—I know what it is like to see yourself as two things: a girl and also an empty and disposable shell.

Somehow, against all odds, we survived. We survived the time as chattel, as child sex workers, as commodities bought and sold. We survived the anger and the fear. We still struggle to survive the anger and the fear.

For me the anger came not only from what was done to me, but also from what I had to do to survive. I was furious with myself for the times I accepted affection from monsters. I loathed the part of me that gave up on God. I was consumed by thoughts of the girls I could not save. My anger of the violence done to me was surpassed by my anger at myself.

The anger was matched by fear. As a child the battle for survival was so fierce that there was little room to feel afraid. Now fear rises up in me where it couldn't before. It is fear of others knowing who I really am. It is the fear that my past defines my present. It is fear that no one could possibly love me if they knew what I had to do in order to survive. The hatred and the fear together created a cloud of blackness that often overcame me.

The darkness was so thick and impenetrable that it made it feel unbearable to be in the world. It weighed me down and made me wish I had never survived the years of abuse at all. My world could be so black that it made believing that light even existed impossible. In order to survive the darkness I had to begin to heal.

Healing is not an easy road, not for me, not for anyone. We all need someone to witness our stories and to hold the light when we can no longer see it. Hope can be elusive, oftentimes seeming just out of reach. It is hard to say, "I deserve healing and hope." And harder still to believe it. That is what makes it so important to find people who remind us.

I am here to remind you with my words, but you need to find someone—anyone—who will listen to the whole truth of your life and treat you with the respect and hope that your survival demands.

You deserve someone to reassure, witness, and shine a light of hope upon your life.

And if not for yourself, allow that light of hope to shine for all of the other nameless and faceless children who are surviving what we have survived.

In sisterhood,
Kathleen Ahern

Melissa Dey Hasbrook

ATTIC

Spider lives under the skylight
weaves and waits for prey

a square of light revolves
east to west

and when Sun is high south
it is calm

in the eye of quiet
I lay naked and say

Sun stroke my skin
Spider riddle me with webs

the long storm has passed
I trade hate for hope

Juliet November

FEMININE WILES

*This piece is dedicated to femmes of all
genders who have survived—and our
sisters and brothers who did not.*

Femininity has always attracted all manner of predators to me.

I'm eight when the first adult male sticks his tongue down my throat and unzips his pants.

Nine when the elderly neighbor invites me and my friends over to his apartment only to realize he isn't wearing pants. Or underwear.

Ten when I walk by a car near the abattoir behind my house and hear a low voice say to me, "You wanna get inside?"

Twelve when my grandfather picks me one night and not my sister. I never know why.

So by thirteen it's too fucking much and the girl in me attempts to go underground.

My cash-poor high-femme mom doesn't understand why I haven't followed in her footsteps. She tells me hopefully, "You're allowed to start wearing makeup." I take up shoplifting makeup that I won't wear. Later she buys me lingerie for Christmas—a lacy green babydoll. The slip sits in my drawer for years till it disappears.

I disappear.

To some extent it works. No one at school notices me in my big sweaters and jeans and glasses with my initials monogrammed into the corner. No boy at school will be seen with me.

But it also fails. I am still shoved into a phone booth by a guy screaming that he wants to hurt the bitch dyke. That would be me—the still-straight fifteen year old. Creeps on the street grab my tits, my ass, my cunt. I get followed, stared at, cat-called a whore, a cunt, a dyke, a slut no matter what I do. The boys at school joke loudly about how much beer they'd have to drink before they'd bother to rape me, and one cool summer night, a guy with a gun chases me and my two best friends down the street screaming that he's going to kill us. When the cops find him, they shrug and say, "He was just playing around. Boys will be boys."

I am scared all the time. By seventeen, I sleep with a knife under my pillow. The most important thing I know about being a woman is that is makes me prey. I don't know what to do to feel safe. My first choice— kill the men—doesn't seem that feasible, though I inhale every man-hating radical feminist tract I can find.

So at eighteen I erase all further evidence of my femininity. What has for five years been a sort of soft androgyny becomes masculinity. I only wear combat boots, hand-me-down chinos, and plaid shirts. Off comes my hair. I start to hear things like "you're such a pretty girl, if only you'd…" and I am delighted. I stop being the kind of girl who seduces Roman Catholic virgins and get a monogamous boyfriend.

I thought that if I could disappear as a woman, I could become safe. That still didn't work, so I tried disappearing from men. At twenty-one I come out into the fantasy-safety world of lesbianism, where I feel hidden from men. Slowly, tentatively over the years I let my femininity come back out. Newly single, I sign up to lap dance at my first women and trans bathhouse. I'm so terrified that I have refused to practice in front of anyone unless it is my lover and she is blindfolded. I nearly throw up from fear the night before.

I get there and a short, voluptuous blonde says, "Oh great, you're here now, I could really use a break."

"Okay, uh, I wasn't supposed to start till later and uh, I…I'm not changed yet."

"Oh here, you can wear this," she says and pulls off the one tiny scrap of clothing she has on, then tosses it to me.

I'm dying of fear, but I control my shaking enough to change and start sliding myself up and down over the hot, brown-eyed butch who is slowly losing her cool underneath me. She licks her lips and says, "Can I touch you, baby? I can tell you want me to."

I don't, actually. So, referring to the clearly posted rules of the feminist bathhouse, I say, "No." She puts her hands down. With a rush, I feel it—*I am the one in charge.* I am nearly naked, sexy, feminine, and Still. In. Charge. Nothing will ever be the same again.

I know without a doubt that I am femme, but while in hiding, my girl hadn't learned anything about *pleasure* and femininity. I discover accessories, eyeshadow, sparkly things, tits, ass, pink, and crying. I get my nineteen-year-old sister to help me buy my first pair of high heels. Since she is a stripper, going to "her shoe store" means that when I choose the smallest heels they have, I still stumble out of there in four inches. I manage to get two blocks before I can't walk and put my big boots back on.

First I learn that femininity can be fun. Then that it is a tool. And as the song goes, "Any tool is a weapon if you hold it right."

Weapon #1

If you're looking at me as a sex object, you can pay me for it. Because now I charge. I don't give it out for free so much anymore since I found out this shit is powerful.

Weapon # 2

I'm at a summer party for a straight friend in my prettiest lavender mini-dress. I get cornered in the kitchen by two mildly drunk white guys with plastic beer cups in their hands. They're increasingly overbearing and eventually White Boy #1 leans in and jokingly pinches my ass. He and his friend chuckle. Before I've thought about it, I've reached out, grabbed hold of both his nipples and twisted them. Hard. I may or may not say, "You'll pay for that."

A look of profound shock crosses his face, followed quickly by confused rage. He stares at my breasts and says, "I…want to do that to…you." I say, "But you *can't*," and take a step back for good measure. His friend and I both laugh while White Boy #1 stands there, mouth gaping open. Of course he turns out to be a secret masochist and tries unsuccessfully to flirt with me for the rest of the night. But he never puts his hand on me again.

Weapon #3

Many years after that first experiment lap dancing, I'm cycling home from another bathhouse along a gentrifying working-class street in Toronto and a huge SUV pulls up alongside me and slows down. I glance over. A guy leans out the window, smiling and trying to get my attention. I realize they are uniformed cops and one of them is talking to me. I shiver and quickly decide to try out "cute" because I've seen it work for middle-class white girls.

"Sorry, what was that? A red? Oh you mean I should have a red light on my bike? Oh I know! I keep forgetting to get one!"

"Oh, no, honey," he says flirtatiously, "you ran a red light back there."

"Oh?"

"Yeah, and you know what you get for that, sweetie?"

"Um…what?" I say, now forcing a smile on my face.

"A spanking," he says and slowly mimics a spanking while smiling and leering at me.

Everything slows down. It's 3 a.m. I have a backpack filled with sex toys, latex gloves, and a trashy slip. I'm wearing a short skirt and heels, biking past deserted alleyways. I don't want to know how the story ends if I'm pulled over and "invited" into their unmarked SUV. I keep smiling while my eyes go cold and hard. I have a split second to come up with something that will keep me safe. When the answer comes, I don't like it, but I'm grateful.

I giggle.

Then, gazing into his hateful little pig eyes, I bite my lip, slowly and seductively, dripping with the imitation of desire. It's a calculated risk. The cop smiles, smugly satisfied. They continue to follow me, leaning out the window, harassing me—until they speed off in another direction.

The moment they're out of sight, I stop my bike dead, take a breath and feel a wave of fear pound through me. I wonder if the cop liked my flirtation—or the fear he saw in my eyes. I feel scared, and in a dirty way, victorious and proud: scared that my working-class femininity has always made me a target, and proud that I have finally honed the skill of protecting myself through its artful use. I did it. I brought out my girl and with every means I have, I am protecting her.

My friend Leah says, "Sometimes you're so busy surviving you forget you have." That night, high from a night of parading around in my short skirt and candy apple red heels and giving head at the glory holes, I remember that I have survived. I am the matador who takes the red flag of my pretty dress and turns it into a cloak.

Femininity is a choice to be myself, even though it puts me in danger. I know how many queers think that being femme is complicit though. They look upon our divine and chaotic femininities and see them as normative, boring, conservative, straight, or just confusing. They say we're shallow, drama, too much, too sexual, too angry, too emotional—even as they come to us for safe space to be these very things.

They think this must be the easy choice. *Easy.* Because a life lived under constant gender violence is natural, obvious, and inevitable—if it happens to feminine people.

But I see you, my dearest femmes. I see your defiance, your courage, your strength, your softness, your sweetness and humor, your wisdom, how badass you are in the face of all this. I worship you and am honored to call myself your sister.

To be feminine, we have had to learn how to use an arsenal of weapons, to be ready and to never let the risks stop us from loving and from loving our femininities. The older I get, the higher my heels and the more tender my heart. From my femme sisters and brothers—I find new ways to navigate the world and honor our precious divinity. If I can handle being alone in a client's home, know how to assess and de-escalate, shut down every sleazeball who's ever thought my pretty dress made me his property, then I can handle the queers who think I just don't understand my own fucking liberation.

I survived.

And in every moment of vulnerability, every swing to my step, every hustle I work, is evidence that I continue to survive. After a long hibernation, my femme emerged and she is not going back into hiding—so I keep my cunt open, my skirts short, and my heels sharp.

Family Ties

LETTER 10: FIFTY-EIGHT YEARS

Dear Sister,

I think it's important for you to know that I am sixty-five years old and have carried this "secret" since I was seven years old. As an adult, I recognize that I was lucky: no penetration, and my mother protected me. She did not leave my dad, but she made sure that I knew his action was his sickness and was not in any way my fault. She talked to me. She made sure I knew that I'd never have to be alone with him again. I understood to be always watchful, always on guard. I never felt any guilt, but even now, all these years later I cannot talk or write about what happened that day without a torrent of tears.

Before that awful day, I was definitely a "daddy's girl," my parents' only child. After that day we pretended it never happened, and it was never spoken of again. I was never left home alone with my father until I was nearly college age. I recognize that now, but I'm not sure that I didn't recognize that somehow when I was growing up.

I never trusted him again. I never liked him again. I was always afraid of him, and I've never forgiven him for not apologizing, or attempting to explain, or trying to do something that would ensure that I would be okay. Three failed marriages tell me that even today I need counseling, and I'm not okay.

I was a grown woman with a child of my own before my heart understood why my mother hadn't left my dad, why she didn't divorce him right then and there. My mother had grown up very poor and she worked very hard, but my dad was the breadwinner. My mother worked for the material things she hadn't had growing up. It was many years before my mother explained that she was afraid that she would not have survived without the financial stability that my dad provided. She had also been afraid that I would have been taken from her if she hadn't stayed married.

My poem below was written twenty-two years ago. I hope it helps somehow.

CHAPTER ONE, PARAGRAPH FIVE

Black & blue & ugly red were my colors
until I was nine.
He took me in bed like I was mother;
rain came from my eyes every time.
The county found out & fumed.
Boy, I hated that woman:
Her questions & stares & sh sh . . .
My childhood was gone.
I spent years inside myself,
Locked, like in a prison cell.
I made home within myself;
I still visit there.

Most times I want to stay
Join Mother in swirling blue irises;
See my daddy across the water
that sweeps him from my mind
So I'll remember to hate him;
Keep it fresh like popcorn & bread.
I wished him to death as a child.
Now he's obliged & I feel much better off.
No longer am I afraid.

Bless you,
Anonymous

Mattilda Bernstein Sycamore

LETTER 11: I CAN'T LEAVE THE BROTHERS OUT

Dear Sister/Brother,

I can't leave the brothers out, not just because
some of them are our sisters, too, not just because
I was a brother and I was abused, alone, a broken
toy, thought I was evil, didn't want to die, shut it all
out. And then, when I remembered, I looked for
resources and there were none: there were resources
for how to recover your masculinity, resources that
showed you how to become a man even though your
father had raped you. But I didn't want to become a
man, ever. I saw the way that masculinity created the
walls I was trying to escape, facilitated the violence,
obliterated the souls of so many faggots and sissies
and queens like myself and not like myself.

I can't leave the brothers out, not just because
some of them are our sisters too, but because some
of them were our sisters, and are now our brothers, building masculinity into something we can
live with, celebrate, challenge, and transform. I can't
leave the brothers out, not just because some of
them are our sisters, too, but because even the bullies
on the playground and in the boardroom, the ones
who succeed in wielding the tools of domination,

some of them too were beaten and bent and broken, tortured and tormented, raped and abused and left to ask why, why am I here, why go on, why?

I am not invoking the disastrous rhetoric that says we are all the same—we are never all the same. Yes, some of the children who master the rules grow into cops and soldiers and politicians and prison profiteers, furthering the violence that continues generation after generation, and they must be held accountable. But still, if we are ever to get out of this relentless cycle of violence building violence into violence, we must include everyone who once looked up from that childhood place of violation, unable to even ask for help, I need help here, can you help?

I believe in accountability. Sometimes it's the only thing I believe in. So often we are left without home or hope, or left only with home as that place of torture, a trap, and hope as something we can hardly even imagine. I know that when I first reached for The Courage to Heal and saw oh, it's not for me, but still it was, and still it kept telling me that, no, it was for women only, and yet still. Hold me, that's what the book was saying—no, hold me—that's what I was saying.

Can you hold me now? I can hold you, until this embrace becomes something other than what we remember, what we dare not remember.

Dear Sister/Brother, I do believe that in order to unlearn the violence, we must unlearn it in all spaces, even the most radical or challenging or intimate or supposedly unharmed or holy, unholy. We need to hold ourselves accountable, not just the ones who harm us—especially in our redefined and recreated spaces. And yes, when the ones who harm us are us.

What do you do when every time you're held you are held down, forced into that familiar position of absence, pain and terror, body split open while you wonder if this time you will die, is this the time? Childhood: something I will never experience, never escape. My father's eyes. My mother?

I was a boy who was not a boy; no one would allow me the space I needed to create something outside of violence. Let's open up that space now. Yes, we need to redefine the world that only holds us to crush us; yes, we need to unlearn the legacy of those parents and lovers and so many others who leave us without a soft place between here and the sky; yes, we need to hold all of this so that we can change, grow, heal, and instigate.

One day maybe we will all belong.

LETTER 12: OH, EVIL DAY!

Dear Sister Survivor,

I need to tell you some things. Some things I've never told anybody. And some things that were shared with me.

I don't know if you've seen the movie *Peter Pan*, but there's a scene in there where the evil Captain Hook clutches his heart and falls to the ground, gasping, "Oh, evil day!" He is looking into the sky, and sees what I see: a girl and boy dancing together, dancing apart, twirling in and out and between each other, holding hands for the first time, smiling together, fairy dust swirling around them. Delighting in the joy of the other. Dancing on air…in love. Hook is jealous. He is seeing what he has never been a part of, what he has never had. He is aching. Clutching his heart so it doesn't break.

My daughter has reached that time. That time when she's spending more and more of her life away from us. Most times I am terrified for her. She will never reach an age when she's safe. When the threat is no longer there. And as she grows further and further away from us, there is less I can do to protect her, to help her. To make sure she is safe.

And yet…

She is tall and beautiful and her father actually talks to her about her period and her new breasts forming. One day she demanded to know when her father and I were going to finally buy her a bra. No embarrassment, no shame. Just general almost-teen but still mostly child outrage that her needs haven't been met instantaneously.

For weeks she has come home, fluttery and happy, brimming over with excited chatter, laughing loud and long at jokes that aren't even that funny. Her father and I haven't entirely understood what is going on—it's not that she's never been cheerful, but more that our daughter doesn't *giggle*. She punches her brother and climbs trees and very sensibly tells on any child who steps out of line. She's a diva. A Queen Diva. And Queen Divas don't giggle!

But then one day she told me her teacher had re-arranged desks again. And now she was sitting next to a particular boy. A boy she's liked for a long time. And suddenly the glowing cheerfulness made sense. The fairy dust swirling around her, elevating her into a world I've never known, choked me. It made her presence toxic to me. Every day I grew more and more angry with her, until I could hardly tolerate being in the room with her.

Oh, evil day!

I am Hook and I fall to the ground, clutching my heart, trying to keep all the pieces from falling out of my body.

***

His kiss was the first kiss I'd ever received. And it came afterward. After I had survived every-thing. He got up to leave, and kissed me. I was so shocked, so thoroughly inducted into the "don't hurt anybody's feelings, be a good girl" ideology that even after he did what he did to me—I didn't want to hurt his feelings by not kissing him back. It wasn't because I felt any compassion for him. It was that, in a moment of stress, I fell back on what had been trained into me: be a good girl. Good girl was my autopilot mode, I knew it so well.

As he leaned in to kiss me—my body rebelled, I started to turn my head, but my mind caught me. *Whoops! Don't hurt his feelings! That will hurt his feelings; don't do that!* I turned my face back to his to meet the kiss, then pulled away quickly. I had done my job. I had not hurt his feelings. And now I needed to get away. That kiss is the moment I remember. That kiss. After everything he did to me.

***

I still, after all this time, have an incredibly difficult time talking about what happened. I turned this letter in to the editor of this anthology past the due date because although I knew I wanted to write something, my fingers wouldn't work when I sat at the computer. My voice only worked in dreams— long terrifying dreams about nothing really, but about everything. A girl with no brain, swamped in bright colors. A girl alone, locked up, happy. I'd wake up gasping like they do in the movies—my heart jamming into my chest, my life partner patting me on the back, only half awake.

I just wanted everything to go away. I've been fascinated about how a lobotomy would free me. How happy to no longer have the pressure of what even I don't understand sneaking through my fingers, slipping in and out of the words I write, breaking my heart every time I look at the brilliance of my daughter…

It is not my fault.

It would've still happened if I were smarter, tougher, angrier, nicer…

It's not my fault.

It's not your fault either.

Nothing you could've done could've changed what happened.

But I know you know what I've spent a huge amount of my life since the assault thinking about:

How could things have been different?

At first, I answered with an emphatic "I never ever would report that ever again. Ever." (I'm not even gonna tell you about the "I never should've worn that" victim-blaming I did.) But over the years that answer shifted. I read feminist texts on rape, talked to other survivors, started to question all the thoughts that were once so automatic. I heard about something called "grooming." Grooming is what a sexual predator does to younger inexperienced people—grooming them to believe that the sex they have with or for the predator is normal.

I started to realize that everything about US culture is grooming. Grooming each of us in different ways—some of us are groomed to be the bad sluts that nobody will ever believe, others of us are groomed to be the popular girl that never has problems—I was groomed to be a good girl. To be considerate of other people's feelings. To not make a fuss. To deal with things until they couldn't be dealt with anymore. Then to disappear, rather than make a big fuss. Don't embarrass. Don't call attention to yourself.

Don't cry when it hurts.
Don't scream when you're scared.
Love is earned, not given.
Love is for good girls.

Do you know how many times I was threatened when I was spanked? I'd cover my butt with my hands to protect myself and was given extra spankings. Extra spankings until I learned that you don't protect yourself when you're being hurt. And that you're being hurt because we love you. Good girls listen to their parents and do what they're told.

So, I want to be a good girl, right? And I want to be loved, right?

There are so many things that groom us to think that what happens to us is normal. There isn't one single thing that you can point to and say, for example—oh, if my parents hadn't forced me to eat carrots when I didn't want to, I never would've been assaulted! But when you work through the endless years of being trained to set aside natural human instincts or that those natural human instincts are something to ignore instead of protect, it all leads up to some really shitty conclusions.

Clean your plate!
Let that baby cry it out!
You're spoiling her!
Spare the rod…
She was such a good, quiet baby!
Don't you roll those eyes at me!
Sit still!
She never causes me any trouble at all!

I got love by being quiet. Being good. Not causing problems. Groomed to consider other people's feelings as I was being hurt. Groomed to think that was normal.

A man thought that he could kiss me after he assaulted me. Because in a heteropatriarchal culture like in the US, you can abuse somebody and love them at the same time. You can honestly believe that the abuse you inflict *is* love. And those of us being hurt are groomed to submit.

It's not my fault.

It's not your fault.

You and me? We're survivors.

I would like to say I have the answers to rape and sexual assault and violence. I don't. Half the time, I don't read the news, and I've long since stopped reading feminist writings on sexual violence. It's so overwhelming, so terrifying—and it's not going to end, not in my lifetime. It's happened to you, to me, to most women I know, to most feminine identified people I know. It's happened to many men I know.

I will die never having raised my hands to the heavens, glorying in freedom. But what I have learned is that you can fight the grooming. You can fight the normalcy of it all. It's not normal what happened to us. It's not normal, and it will never be right no matter how hard they try force us to believe it. It's not normal. And it's not our fault.

As I watch my daughter growing up, I see her going through something beautiful and tender and brilliant—and delicate. Something that is sifting through my fingers like water. She is growing up. She is becoming a sexual being. She is learning what she desires, what she loves. Up until now, I've told her what she can love and desire. She is breaking away from her father and me. She dances on air and I am jealous. The air she dances on is protected by loving fairies—her friends, her aunties, her grandparents, her teachers—me. She has what I never did.

Oh…evil day!

She has found herself….love.

This child loves herself. Somehow as her mother crawled on the ground clutching her broken heart, this child learned to love herself. She is not safe forever. She will never outgrow the threat. But every day, one step at a time, she is helping a whole community to normalize the idea of a new kind of love. A love that holds a child learning how to dance on her own as precious. Worth protecting.

This is a world I have never known…but am getting to know. For so long I was Hook, standing on the outside, looking in—knowing only the hurt, the anger, and the devastation that so many of us are not held precious by the world. It was my daughter who invited me in. Who let me know that her world could not happen without me. That it is possible to dance again, even after you've been hurt.

I want you to know the same thing.

Because, you and me?

We're survivors.

May you be safe. May you be happy. May you be free.

Love,
brownfemipower

Dorla Harris

LETTER 13: THE AFTERSHOCK

Dear Sisterfriend,

I have not lived your experience, but I am a part of it. I am an aftershock. I am the worst-case scenario.

I am the product of years of sexual abuse. But I am also your strength. My soul is made up of pieces of your strength and survival. There is a piece of me that comes from the first time he touched you. There is a piece of me that comes from the first time he broke your trust and tore into your being. There is a piece of me that comes from every time he repeated this act. There is a piece of me for every time you felt the need to lie, risking your own safety, to protect others around you.

There is a piece of me for when you told someone the truth and a piece for when you were forced to tell everyone the truth by the fetus growing in your teenage body. There is a piece of me that comes from the insults and abuse from your mother emerging out of her own feelings of anger, helplessness and shame. Part of me is made up of the misplaced feelings of guilt you felt as your rapist and step-father fled, leaving your half siblings abandoned and confused. A big piece of me is made of your journey through pregnancy and labor. The emotions behind all of these pieces of me fit together to make me whole. The most important piece of me comes from the fact that you are still here, living, giving life to other children who you chose to create and are loving as best you can, including me.

Your actions are your own and do not reflect the unjust and violent actions that were forced upon you. Your determination to live and dedicate so much of yourself to allow me to live beyond your suffering is far reaching. Your survival has been my life source.

I thank you. Your openness to taking on life, love, happiness, and hope has most shaped my soul. Words really are not enough. Life. Love. Happiness. Hope. They are all bigger than the names they bear.

Know that I live and love with the strongest pieces of your experience fueling my every step. Your strength is behind every goal I achieve. The pieces, filled with your strength, allow me to survive my own traumas and look forward to the future. Without your strength, there would not have been a future for me.

Aftershocks can sometimes work to shake loose the harmful toxins that need to be released. The process of this release is extremely painful, but the purity that replaces the toxins is healing. What began as the worst-case scenario has evolved into the best result. I am living a full and happy life through your grace. Now you can take pieces of me to give you the strength to lead you beyond a past that was never rightfully yours to begin with.

Much love, respect, and gratitude,
Your child

Amita Y. Swadhin

LETTER 14: AMITA'S FINE

Dear Sister,

When I was thirteen years old, I was just starting to confront the reality of surviving eight years
of rape and other forms of sexual, physical, and
emotional abuse by my father. I felt utterly alone.
I read everything I could find about child sexual
abuse and father-daughter incest, searching for a
guidebook that would tell me what to do. I lingered
for hours in the self-help aisle of every bookstore
and library I entered. I wanted so badly to be
"normal," to move on quickly with my life. But I
learned the hard way—interpersonal violence, particularly sexual violence committed against you by
someone you know and love, changes you forever.
And if you truly want to get well, there is no going
around your feelings and memories—you have to
go *through* them.

Today, more than twenty years after I first disclosed, I am at a new stage in my healing process. I
love my life, I feel present to all that life has to offer,
and I feel gratitude to be so alive. Most of all, I can
feel—both physically and emotionally. This is nothing short of a miracle to me.

This is my attempt at explaining how I got here. What I have to say is based only on my own journey; I do not claim to speak for all survivors. Yet perhaps hearing my story will in some small way help you in your healing process. Perhaps it will help you to hear that healing, though never easy and never over, is possible. We cannot change our experiences of violence, and we cannot escape the toll that those experiences take on our body, mind, and spirit. But we can decide who and how we want to be in this world. And in shaping our selves, we can claim our power.

I spent most of the first thirteen years of my life completely numb and completely pretending. I was four years old the first time my father raped me; I don't remember much of life before violence. The violence continued for eight years, including being raped at least once a week. Numbing out was a coping mechanism, achieved by filling my time with every after-school activity and honors class I could find, reading a ton of fantasy stories (escape via unicorns and dragons and portals to other worlds!), playing video games, listening to music, watching a *lot* of TV, and trying hard to spend as much time with other kids as possible. Pretending was another coping mechanism—I had to convince everyone around me (friends, teachers, neighbors, relatives) that everything was okay. I was such a good actor that I had most believing everything was great!

When I finally told my mother about the abuse I'd experienced, I was thirteen. It was 1991. My father had stopped raping me sometime the year before. I was worried he was raping my sister, or that he soon would. I wasn't sure what I wanted, beyond knowing that I wanted my mother, my sister, and myself to be safe. My feelings about my father were complicated—at some point, I had loved him. After all, he was my father, and he wasn't violent 100 percent of the time—more like 80 percent. But that 20 percent mattered. It was confusing; it was evidence that he was in fact capable of non-violence. Back when I still silently prayed myself to sleep every night, before I became an atheist, I would pray not for him to die or disappear, but simply for him to stop hurting me. But at some point, I can't articulate exactly when, I crossed some threshold emotionally: the rape, the emotional belittling, the yelling, the beating, the constant and unpredictable threat of violence—it was all too much. I stopped loving him, but I still had to live with him, so I didn't even have room to hate him. I spent a lot of time hating myself, though. I was scared that in truth I was a monstrosity, because after all, I was the daughter of a monster. And I was so, so ashamed.

My mother immediately called a friend to get a referral for a therapist. She wanted me to be able to heal, I suppose, and her reflexes were quick (or long overdue, depending on your perspective). Because I was only thirteen at the time, the therapist she called was a mandated reporter. We didn't even know to consider that. And before my father came home from work, before I even had a chance to collapse into my mother's arms and grieve, let alone contemplate what I wanted to do, the New Jersey Division of Youth and Family Services was involved.

Some time in that next week, our house was invaded by social workers. I faced these two white people, a man and a woman, alone in my living room a few times over the next month. I listened to them tell me they understood, since "this happens so often in your culture." I grimaced through their attempts to meet me on what they assumed was my intellectual level, unable to hide my disdain when they insisted on using crude slang for all of the body parts I had been able to spell the proper names of since age five. Yes, I told them, he had stopped abusing me. No, I didn't know why.

My father was ordered out of the house and into a motel so that a more thorough investigation could be conducted. We still saw him on weekends, though, and strangely, we all drove to the courthouse together for questioning. After threatening us again on the ride over, my father went in to see the two white male prosecutors, while I was questioned alone by a white female police officer. She stared at me blankly while I broke down in tears, perfunctorily patted my hand, and said, "You clearly need therapy, but that's not my job. I'm just here to get some answers." I steeled myself then, and looking past her to the one-way glass staring back at me over her shoulder, informed her I had nothing to say until whoever was behind that mirror observing my suitability to take the witness stand showed me the respect of meeting me face to face while sizing me up. That, as they say, was the end of that. Next up, the prosecutors. They told me they were considering prosecuting my mother, too, for endangering my welfare and failing to protect me. My father abused my mother in so many ways for years; the last thing I wanted was for her to be thrown in jail and my sister and I to be separated and placed into foster care. I figured it was better to live with the devil you know than the devil you don't know; when your father beats and rapes you regularly, you just assume strangers will treat you worse. My father admitted to "fondling" me, one time. And I said I had nothing else to add to his statement.

Yes, I lied. It's hard to explain why, but in that moment I did not want my father to go to jail. I did not want the world to know what he had done to me. I did not want to be a media sensation. I just wanted to keep working my way toward college. Besides, my father threatened me and especially my mother every time he saw us. My nine-year-old sister started to hate me for "tearing our family apart." And my mother had always talked so poorly about divorce. I didn't want to be the cause of everyone's suffering. I did not want my father to kill us in retaliation. And I did not want to put words to the horrific acts that he had done to me for eight years. I did not want it to be so real. So I lied.

My father lived with us for another two years after that. In that time, he admitted to my mother and sister, in front of me, what he had done. He never used the word "rape," and no one ever asked. He never apologized. He simply said, "All that is in the past now. It's over, and Amita is fine. Look at her. She does well in school. Besides, I did the same thing to my nieces in India, and they're fine, too. And when I was little, this happened to me, too. The servants, the neighborhood boys, they did this to me. And it's all in the past. I stopped on my own. Now the real problem," he said as he turned to my little sister, "is that Amita and your mother have involved strangers in our family business. We have to do something about that."

His solution was to increase his physical and verbal violence toward all of us. The summer I turned fifteen, my sister and I were on our annual visit to my maternal grandmother's house in Ohio. While we were away, my father started beating my mother every day, throwing her against the wall, holding her by the neck, telling her she was his to kill if he wanted. After sixteen years of marriage, she finally got the courage to leave because she realized she would certainly die if she stayed. She was thirty-four years old when she had my father removed from our house in handcuffs and filed for a restraining order and a divorce.

That next year was my junior year of high school. I tried to stay on track with college preparations—SATs, honors classes, extracurricular activities. With my father out of the house, I finally had room to process everything without constantly worrying about his retaliation. By the end of that school year, my sister had finally grown up enough to understand, and she agreed to our visitation sessions with our father. With this new freedom, I slowly started to move past the numbness and denial to the next classic stage of grief: anger.

As my sensations evolved from the first prickles of indignation to full-on waves of searing rage, I realized that I needed to tell the truth. I realized how much I hated my father, how much I wished for him to be punished with all that I could throw his way. I contemplated killing him, had thought about it many times during my adolescence, every time he put his hands on me. But each time I concluded that the one thing separating me from him was that I was nothing like him. I didn't cause people to suffer.

He was a monster. I was a person. He had taken so much from me already. He had made me into a victim, a raped and broken little girl. I didn't want him to make me a murderer, too. Besides, quite frankly, I was never sure I would actually be able to wound him before he killed me.

After I shared the full details of my survivorship with my mother, we tried to prosecute my father again. I was ready to tell the good cop/bad cop prosecution team the truth, the whole truth, and nothing but the truth, even though I no longer believed in God. Yet the prosecution could not move forward because of double jeopardy.

So I tried to move on with my life. Just about a year after I spoke to my father on the phone for the last time, I packed up my stuff and moved to Washington, DC, for college. I interned at the national Office of Violence Against Women and answered phone calls and letters from desperate women who had lost custody of their children to men who not only abused them, but also raped and sexually assaulted their children. These men were often judges, prosecutors, and police officers—men who were protected by the system that was supposed to hold them accountable. I realized I wasn't the only one the system had failed. I studied the epidemic of child sexual abuse and realized I was far from alone. And I was consumed by my rage. I walked out of an Amnesty International meeting on campus when I realized they were against the death penalty; I wanted nothing more than to see my father killed—it's the only just outcome I could imagine. And yet I knew that desire would be my demise if I fed it; being filled with hate toward my father was only harming myself, given that I couldn't actually harm him. The frustration led to a downward spiral. I tried my best to channel my anger into activism, and in some ways succeeded—I organized Take Back the Night on my campus; I helped amend the college's sexual assault policy; I held the stories of countless friends; I shared my own story countless times. Yet my inability to hold my father accountable tore me apart. I began having writer's block. School, which had always come so easily, began to feel like a burden. I had nightmares, when I could sleep. I failed all of my classes while studying abroad during my junior year, and I nearly dropped out of school. When I returned to the US, I entered therapy and was diagnosed with post-traumatic stress disorder.

I took a leave of absence, moved home, and got a job in New York City working for an organization educating judges and prosecutors about how many adult survivors of sexual violence are re-traumatized by the prosecution process and the criminal legal system. I was still feeling the trauma myself. I was just beginning to connect the dots. And I felt a strong pull to work with young people, to engage in positive and visionary work, to feel like I was helping someone, somewhere, somehow. Mainly because I wasn't sure how to help myself, and I knew I had to keep channeling my anger into *something* positive, lest it consume me or lead to another breakdown. So, soon after I finished my last few undergrad classes, I got a new job—working in New York City public schools through an after-school program engaging youth in civic service and human rights activism.

I was twenty-three years old and working at the edges of the city, so far out that I had to take a train to a bus and then walk to reach the school doors. Nearly 100 percent of the students I worked with were Black (African American or immigrants from Africa or the Caribbean) or Latino (mainly Puerto Rican and Dominican). One of my first assignments was to build a support program for gang-involved boys close to dropping out. Over that first year, I met twice a week with a group of ten boys, all only a few years younger than myself. Many had been incarcerated. All had family members and friends who were incarcerated. Many had seen friends or family members get shot. Some had seen these loved ones die before their eyes. A few were fathers. The first year I started working there, the school was designated an "impact school"—one of the twelve most violent schools in the city—by the mayor, and the number of armed police officers in the building tripled in the name of safety. Many of the teachers in that high school were either white folks who said things to me like, "I can't believe someone as smart as you is wasting your time with the bottom-feeders of our school," or Black middle-class folks who said things like, "What do you expect from those kids? They live in the projects. This is all they're capable of."

Meanwhile, the "toughest" kid in my group (according to the head guidance counselor)—a lanky, dark-skinned eighteen-year-old who had done time at Rikers and was known as a leader in a local gang—sucked his thumb during one-on-one counseling meetings in my office, relaying tales of spending nights on his mother's front steps because she had locked him out of the apartment. He never talked about violence he had experienced. He didn't need to; it was written all over him.

I had no idea how to help these young men. I knew I couldn't save them. But I found I was good at connecting with them. Not in a weird "freedom writers" outsider-savior kind of way. In a way I couldn't have explained at the time but understand now, I saw myself in them. We were all broken but hiding it. Surviving institutional and interpersonal violence against all odds. Faking it all the time. Trying to make it. And in the midst of all this, I learned I was good at creating safe spaces for real talk. I was good at showing them I saw their humanity, their potential, their talent. I loved them, fiercely and unconditionally. And slowly, through that act, I learned to love myself.

I should mention that from the moment I went to college through all the years of working for social justice, I also tried desperately to heal (or at least cope) in many other ways. I read a lot of poetry and essays by queer activists of color, especially women who discussed intimate forms of violence. I traveled, as often and as far as I could. I cultivated friendships and community. I went dancing and sang karaoke. I drank, too much. I read angry and evocative work by other survivors, like *Hothead Paisan: Homicidal Lesbian Terrorist*. I spent a lot of time fantasizing, about everything from revenge-fueled acts of violence against my father to erotic visualizations about various lovers. I learned about my body—what nurtured it, what pleased it, what hurt it. I tried to write creatively. I tried to play the guitar. I tried to cook. I tried to create home with different loved ones— friends and lovers. I read a lot of science fiction and fantasy. I spent a lot of time soaking in all that New York had to offer—museums, musicals, nightclubs, and lots of good restaurants. I think of this entire process as stumbling toward healthiness; it was often three steps forward, two steps back (sometimes three). But it was cumulatively forward, inch by hard-won inch.

I've continued to work with young people of all genders in schools and after-school settings over the past decade. Each organizing campaign or community action—painting a mural in the cafeteria about the need for comprehensive sex education; marching through the neighborhood holding giant puppets and signs against intimate violence; mobilizing on the steps of the Department of Education to demand the removal of cops in schools; doing street theater on the Christopher Street Pier to collect petition signatures in support of a drop-in center for LGBTQ youth; hosting a rally and concert to raise support for the DREAM Act—has empowered me as much as, I'd like to think, it's made a difference in the lives of the youth I've worked with. I am a queer woman of color who grew up struggling middle class. I am "ethnically ambiguous," or so I've been told. I often lived in New York neighborhoods that mirrored the ones in which I worked. And, of course, there was the debilitating rage coursing through me due to my early experiences of trauma. Every time I helped organize against social injustice, every time I helped a young person realize and activate their own power, it channeled that rage and made me feel I was fighting back against all the forms of injustice that had derailed my own youth, in a way that nothing else ever had.

There was a big disconnect in my life, though. I was helping young people name and heal from their experiences of intimate and institutional violence, but for the most part, I wasn't politicizing my own experiences. I kept work and personal life pretty separate when it came to my survivor story. I talked to my therapist, my friends, and my lovers—but I never told anyone all of the details at once of what I had survived. It felt too heavy, too terrifying, too infuriating. I thought I would self-destruct or lose my mind if I dared to speak it all or write it all at once. And so, beneath everything, the rage persisted, eating away at my soul like a slow, simmering cancer.

By the time I got to graduate school, I was teetering on the edge of another breakdown. I had left a verbally and emotionally abusive relationship just months before starting my master's program. I wasn't sleeping much. I wasn't eating right. I was cycling through lovers and glasses of alcohol whenever I wasn't in the library, and I was far from well. I had originally entered grad school to continue my work in public education and youth development from a policy perspective. Yet every time I sat down to calculate a statistics assignment or write a paper, I found my thoughts drifting. The only words I could easily find were about all that I had survived—and I couldn't even put them on paper. I found myself telling anyone who stuck around long enough to listen. I had run from my own story for so long that it had become bottled up inside me, forming an intellectual roadblock that I had to remove in order to move forward. And so, I created *Secret Survivors*, a theater project with Ping Chong & Co. (a performance company I'd worked with in the past), featuring me and other survivors of child sexual abuse telling our stories through dramatic narrative. And I switched my academic focus to child sexual abuse—studying the scope and impact of the epidemic and trying to distill best practices in intervention, prevention, and healing that could be presented as policy recommendations.

I spent my second year of grad school simultaneously writing my narrative out for our script and reading a lot of scientific research about the epidemic of child sexual abuse. I also read publications by INCITE! Women of Color Against Violence and generationFIVE. I read *The Revolution Starts at Home*. And slowly, meticulously, I began to connect the dots in a whole new way. I learned that at least one in four girls and one in six boys would experience sexual abuse by age eighteen. Ninety-three percent of these cases involve abuse by someone well known to the child; up to 47 percent of these cases are perpetrated by a family member. And less than 30 percent of cases are ever reported to authorities. None of that surprised me.

But I was shocked to learn that nearly 50 percent of people who sexually abuse children are themselves under age eighteen. I had spent years trying to unconditionally love every young person who crossed my path, to try to give them something my parents had never given me. Now I had to face the question of whether any of those young people had ever harmed anyone the way I had been harmed. And if so, what did I think should be done with them? I knew from personal experience that the criminal legal system often caused more harm to the survivors seeking justice. Now I connected all that I had learned about how the prison industrial complex disproportionately targets low-income people of color. Now I learned that every year over 200,000 adults and children in US detention are sexually abused; in most cases, the perpetrators are corrections staff. I also considered the fact that people who sexually molest or even rape a child do not receive lifelong sentences.

Even if we could somehow identify everyone who has ever sexually abused a child, what would it mean to subject them all to a system that disproportionately punishes people who are low-income people of color, potentially subject them to sexual assault in prison, and release them after a relatively short while, probably more harmed and full of rage and violence than they were to begin with? Moreover, what would it mean that 50 percent of these people would be *children* under the age of eighteen? I realized that I would not wish rape and other forms of sexual assault on anyone, not even my father, given how well I understand the deep and profound ways this particular form of violence rends a person's spirit, and I became convinced that we needed to find solutions to this epidemic outside of the criminal legal system.

The creative work I was doing through Secret Survivors also forced me to reexamine the experiences and cast of characters of my childhood in a whole new way. One of my role models, Bayard Rustin (a Black gay man who was the strategist behind much of the Civil Rights Movement, including the March on Washington), once said, "Take power away from those who misuse it—at which point they become human too." In thinking about how child abuse could truly and permanently end, I had to humanize my father, to consider the factors that have led him to commit such atrocious acts of violence for such a long part of his life.

I took out a photo album I still have, one that we hid away when he came to the house to collect his belongings with a police escort. It holds old family photos of him as a boy in India. These are the only photos I can look at of him without feeling triggered, nauseated, and enraged. And for the first time in my life, I found myself remembering his story about being raped as a little boy while I looked at those pictures. And I saw my child self in his empty, dissociated gaze, the serious set of his mouth. I realized that there had been a time in my father's life that he was a victim, not a perpetrator. And for whatever reason, he had come out of those years wreaking havoc on all the women and girls he had access to. Maybe he didn't have loving parents. Maybe he never had friends. Maybe he was even more alone than I had been all those years; after all, I had a younger sister, a loving grandmother and aunt who I visited every summer, and a constant collection of close friends and playmates. Despite all the violence I had endured, I could look back at my childhood and remember many happy moments. Perhaps he couldn't say the same. The boy staring back at me from the photo certainly didn't look like he had ever known love or joy. For the first time in my life, I felt sorry for him. I pitied him. And I felt the weight on my shoulders lighten ever so slightly.

Don't get me wrong: I have *not* forgiven my father. Some acts are truly unforgivable. But I have compassion for him, through understanding his origins as a broken little boy. He, too, is a survivor.

And this compassion has been a gateway for my own deeper healing. Through releasing some of the white-hot anger at my father, I have created an emotional clearing to feel something else. And what I have uncovered there is a deep, deep well of sorrow, guilt, and shame. I didn't realize that just below the surface of my anger lay so many negative feelings about myself; I now better understand why so many of my coping mechanisms, rooted in these feelings, are actually self-destructive. I am now working on healing those wounds and transforming these patterns. Having compassion for my father has opened a path for me to forgive myself.

In the past two years, I have given up alcohol, practiced yoga, received acupuncture, and engaged in other somatic healing techniques. I have built intentional healing community with other queer people of color who are trauma survivors. I have apologized to my sister for all of the ways that I took my abuse out on her; engaging in a deeper level of healing forced me to reexamine and hold myself accountable for the physical and emotional violence I perpetrated against her as a way of releasing some of the violence that was being done to me. We have worked hard on our relationship, and I think we're on the path to becoming friends, one step at a time. I have drawn much clearer boundaries with friends and past lovers, ones that prioritize wellness and interdependence. And I have created a clearing in my life to have the healthiest and most joyful romantic partnership I've ever engaged in. I honestly do not think any of this would have been possible had I not arrived at a place of compassion. I know I am on the healing path that is right for me.

Of course, I'm still left with some very hard questions. Though I have compassion for my father and believe that the prison industrial complex is not a solution to the violence he has perpetrated, I certainly don't think he deserves to be roaming free in society. He is remarried, has two teenage children, and lives forty minutes away from my family. He has made it clear in so many ways that he is completely unremorseful. I know for a fact that he has raped and/or molested at least eight different young women and girls in his lifetime, and the real number is probably higher. I have no reason to believe that he has stopped committing this kind of harm. What is to be done with someone like my father? The question often eats at me, keeps me up many nights.

I have slowly come to terms with the fact that I will not find the answer on my own. Whatever true accountability looks like, I know I cannot achieve it alone. The conditions that allowed my father to rape and abuse me were bred in interdependence at all levels; the violence did not happen in a vacuum. His extended family, our South Asian community, the church, the temple, even the police and prosecutors—all of these forces worked together to create this tale.

And so, I find myself engaged in transformative justice work, exploring community-based solutions to intimate violence with my friends and colleagues. Trying to hold people who have caused harm accountable without relying on the criminal legal system. Trying to provide support both to the people who have been harmed and the people who have committed harm, because I finally understand that people who commit violence are not monsters;

chances are that at their root, they too are survivors. I finally see the harm I have committed in the past, and I am able to take responsibility for it and work on my healing and transformation. And I do not believe I am a better person than anyone else. I believe that anyone can change, anyone can heal. In theory.

I have hope that together we can figure out a better way to deal with the violence that is woven into every layer of our individual and collective lives. And most of all, I hope that you, too, find your healing path.

With love,
Amita

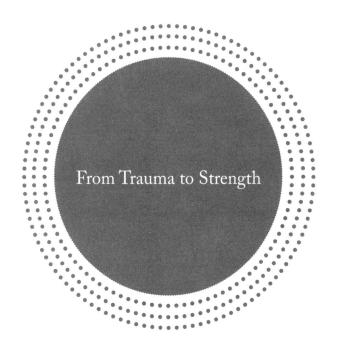

From Trauma to Strength

Brooke Benoit

SURVIVING BIRTH

Cradling a strangely endearing plush toy pelvis in her hands, the childbirth instructor had just asked our group, "What do you expect of your labor?" I hadn't thought as far ahead as labor. This was my first pregnancy and I was keenly sensitive to every minute change occurring in and on my body. I was all consumed with the actual pregnancy. I was exhausted. And mildly nauseous, and a little hungry— yet always having the presence of some indigestion. I had a wintertime heat rash in New York and another weird rash on my eyelids, which my hip co-workers had mistaken for me trying out some retro new-wave trend with pink shadow. Being fashionable wasn't a pressing issue for me in those harried months; "pregnant" was all I felt and thought about.

While some of the couples in the class had a great deal to say, all I could hear in my head was "I expect to live." Finally, when my turn came, that is what I said. I expect to live. After a prolonged pause of silence in which I was intensely stared at by a room full of strangers, the instructor asked me to elaborate. I begrudgingly explained that "with all the medical technology and stuff, I expect to live." My husband has my unconditionally loyal love for even less eloquently grunting out in his turn, "Well, uh, yeah. That." I was surprised that no one else seemed to be remotely freaked out by labor like I was. The couples all shared shiny-happy feelings of what they were expecting: to have their partners support and coach them through the delivery, to use breathing and meditation techniques instead of pain relievers—to have fabulous and empowering birth experiences.

I didn't expect to puke. I started puking with the first notable signs of labor—which were simply stronger, more painful contractions than the little ones I had been having for days—and I continued vomiting for hours. My water broke, or "partially broke," but when and how much I wasn't sure because I was puking when it happened. I had been told to try and eat before coming in for delivery, so my husband dutifully and excitedly brought home a complete shawarma and falafel mezze from our favorite kosher spot on Coney Island Avenue. I savored it, helping my husband to devour every bit, as the midwives had advised me to "eat like an athlete" since I was preparing myself to go into hard labor. Before the empty wrappings were gathered up I resumed puking. I puked in the car and at the intake and for hours in the delivery room. My midwife, who had been giving me ice and sips of cool water, finally went against the implicit instructions on my birth plan and offered me something for the nausea—but I would have to be hooked up to an IV to get it. Panic vaguely pulsed through my tired and weakened body. Surely I had expected this to be hard, but the vomiting was rendering me nearly incapacitated. I was worried that I wasn't able to think clearly. The offer for sweet relief had to be weighed against my being on an IV; that would be the first intervention chipping away at my autonomy. My movements would become limited, a snowball effect of interventions could occur in which I would become simply a body without say, made pliable and easy for a medical team to "work on." I wanted to remain in control of what was put in my body, and I wanted to do the labor myself rather than have it done to me.

Where I had once found comfort in the idea of being saved from the pains and uncertainty of labor with the use of medical technology and a thoroughly trained staff, by the time I went in to delivery I understood that medicine would not magically save me. After the birthing classes, I started to accept that the pregnancy would end and that I would have to do the actual labor process. In a last ditch attempt to opt out of labor, I casually mentioned to my husband that maybe I could just have a C-section. He was shocked by this suggestion and reassured me, "It would be better to just have the baby natural, like everyone else, than to be cut into for no reason." I hadn't admitted to him or anyone else that I was completely freaked out by the idea of being in labor; on the surface I didn't even understand that I was unusually frightened. I didn't know where to begin addressing my anxiety, but finally I realized that I had to stop thinking only about the fascinating phenomenon of "pregnancy" and began voraciously reading everything available to me about labor.

I learned that birth was a process that unfolded, and that, when attempting to control the process through unnecessary medical means, both physical and emotional damage could likely occur to the mother and the child. I heard about making a birth plan ahead of time as I would be, well, distracted during the labor process. Care providers could refer to the plan rather than disturb me or force me to make a decision hastily. So I did that and I wrote in it that I didn't want to be given any drugs and not to even offer me any, in case I should buckle. Perhaps I would have reconsidered my rigid stance had I known that anti-nausea meds may be needed, but in my self-led crash course on What to Expect in Labor, I hadn't read about puking.

It wasn't until I was ready to have my second baby that I had learned from Mama Google how vomiting in labor is thought to have a correlation with sex abuse survivors. For that first birth, I was in the dark about how labor can affect sexual abuse survivors; I wasn't able to connect my freaked-outness about labor and my personal history. I had not yet gone through any therapy or healing process. But today, a dozen years and a few more babies later, I can tell you what was freaking me out about anticipating labor: I knew there was going to be a lot of pain and that it would be centered around my vagina. I knew that there was a looming date fast approaching, at which time things were going to happen to my body that I felt I had no control over. I was particularly worried about the ambiguous "pushing thing" that was about to happen, and I foresaw it in my mind as a scene with a room full of blue and white coat-wearing people screaming at me to "Push! Push! Push!" How was it that they would know when I should push but that I might not? How could I prevent not pushing wrongfully and receiving the kind of horrid lacerations and tears I had heard some women describe? Understandably, all that could be enough to cause panic in someone who has survived sexual assault or abuse. I wasn't cognizant that this is what I needed to read about: how sexual abuse can affect a woman in pregnancy, in labor, and post-partum. That was information I could have used.

While I have had six babies over the last fourteen years, I have been given innumerable handouts warning me about the dangers correlated with pregnancy, everything from coffee to cat poop. I've been given practical information about how to prepare my perineal tissue, vaginal muscles, and even my nipples. But I have never been given a handout that told me, "If you are a sex abuse survivor, it is likely that your prior experience may affect you during labor." I remember being given Xerox copies of stuff that really didn't interest or concern me, and being told, "Oh, you can just pass it on to a pregnant friend." As obnoxious as I think that is, I also think that maybe some of that stuff was important for me to read, and my midwives were optimistic that I might get to it later. As I am the "one" in one out of four pregnant women who have experienced sexual trauma, I'm disappointed that none of my care providers saw the importance of addressing my demographic.

Of the six midwifery practices that I used during my pregnancies, I know that if not all, at least some of them did query me about my medical, sexual, and psychological history, for their records. When they asked, I lied. Well, thank you, stranger, but no, I am not ready to talk to you about the most painful period of my life, which up to now I have only discussed lightly with a very few of my most trusted friends. But if you have a handout that you could slip into my little welcome package or perhaps some titles in your suggested reading material, I may just go ahead and take care of myself.

Between my first and second baby, I went into therapy seeking some help to heal myself, likely for the sake of my child. During that time, in midwife and medical journals and on message boards, I read first-person survivor narratives about sex abuse and how it can affect laboring. Later on, as a thirty-nine-year-old woman having her sixth baby, I still felt out of touch with my body and had difficulties discerning hunger, tiredness, or illness. I realized that looking at detailed medical images of the birth process helped me to understand what was happening in my body during labor much more than the common practice of being told how I would feel. My confidence in myself and the process grew tremendously over time as I increased my own knowledge base about pregnancy and especially about labor. Still, that first labor ended much differently than I ever could have imagined.

I had pulled the IV into the bathroom of the labor room and there I hid away from nurses, my husband, my mother, and anyone else passing through the room during the final portion of my labor. My midwife assured me that some women are more comfortable delivering on the toilet and that she could help me do that. That didn't appeal to me; I just wanted to hide away and not be touched or talked to while my baby slowly made his way down my birth canal. I was massaging my own perineum, as I had read this could be comforting (which I found was true), when I felt something firm and very different. His head! Years later I would learn that this was called "crowning," but right then I knew—it was time to push.

With a few good pushes (based on my own timing, not the nurse's or midwife's) he slipped out of my body, and I immediately thought, "That was great!" Amazingly, I likened it to another puke-inducing activity: "That was like a roller coaster," I blubbered to no one in particular. "I want to do it again!"

I have survived six fabulous births and two miscarriages.

Michelle Ovalle

SMOOTH AS SCALES

The memory
always comes to me:
  a snake, green,
  seafoam slither
      over every inch
      of my body, tongue
          flicks everything,
          ignores *no*s,
              hands faintly
              resisting touch.
          I mistake
          the look in its eyes
      for passion
      or love.
  No—
  it is hunger.
He licks
the air between us,
  inches from my face,
  opens his fanged,
      lipless mouth
      and begins
          to swallow me
          whole.

Andrea Harris

FROM ONE SURVIVOR TO ANOTHER

After the rape, I kept what had happened close to my heart like a special secret for a long time, and doing so kept it a part of me. It was only when I started speaking the truth of what had happened to me that I was able to see it as something separate from myself—as something that happened to me, rather than something that I was. For those survivors who feel as though you are defined by the violence, *none* of us, including you, are defined by what has been done to us. We define ourselves. Let that secret go: hold it out apart from you so that it can be seen for what it really is.

Because I chose to drive my rapist home and had kissed him earlier that night, I wondered if I deserved what had happened. I thought I should have been smarter. But now I know that my intellect is not the problem: the choice someone made to rape me is the problem. By accepting that I would do the same thing today—that I would drive home an apparently intoxicated acquaintance to keep him off the road and keep him safe—I reclaimed my sense of who I am. If you are wondering how you should change, *you* don't need to change. Fight to hold onto who you are.

As I felt the breath leaving my body, I stopped fighting him. And when he lifted the pillow off my face, I didn't scream or cry again. More than anything, I wanted to be able to get off that bed and walk away when he was done, so, when he insisted that I "liked it," I agreed. And I did walk away, right after I convinced him that I had liked it so much that I would come back the next night so that he could do it to me again. Because I did those things, I thought I wasn't a real victim, let alone a real survivor. I believed that I was complicit in what had happened to me. Now I know that how I survived has nothing to do with the truth of what was done to me. If you are questioning what you did and how you survived, please stop. *Whatever* you did to survive is the right thing.

Because the man who raped me told me how beautiful I was and how much he loved me while he was raping me, it took me a long time before I could hear someone tell me I was beautiful or tell me how much they loved me without cringing. But today I can. If you are cringing when people who care about you tell you they love you and remind you how beautiful you are, call upon your righteous anger and don't let the ones who hurt us take love and beauty from us, too.

After the rape, most people I knew seemed eager to believe his story of consensual rough sex, rather than my story of rape. The woman police detective to whom I first shared my story commented that the bite marks and bruises on my neck looked like evidence of "passionate love-making" to her. The mutual acquaintances I shared with the man who raped me began referring to me as "that crazy freaky bitch"— much like he had done when he told the police that I was lying about the rape to cover up the truth that I liked "rough sex." After the police initially dismissed the rape as a "he said, she said" case, my friends and family told me I should just forget about it and move on with my life. It seemed to be easier for everyone if I just stopped talking about it. In that silence, my reality—the truth of what had happened to me—was lost. When everywhere you turn, people are discounting your words, doubting your truths, and denying your reality, you begin to feel crazy. For me, sanity came though refusing to be silent.

I am one of the few: the man who raped me would eventually plead guilty to his crime and be sentenced to prison. However, for me, justice came before the cell door finally closed—when the man who raped me admitted that what he had done to me *was* rape. You must decide what is justice for you. Just know that you are not crazy. You are believed. And you deserve justice.

After the rape, a woman at my church who was friends with the mother of the man who raped me told me what a "good boy" the man who raped me had always been and then instructed me to pray for him. It took me a while to understand that the soul of my rapist is not my responsibility and to instead take responsibility for my own spiritual well-being and self-forgiveness. I had always thought of myself as the kind of woman who would not "let" herself be raped and would instead fight back, so I had to forgive myself for becoming a victim. However, I also had to forgive myself for believing that I could ever be defined by what someone else did to me. At the end of self-forgiveness was the realization that I didn't "let" myself be raped. I am still that woman who would fight back: I fought back by making it out of there alive. If you are wondering about your obligation to the well-being of the person who raped you, you have none: you owe your rapist nothing. But you owe yourself forgiveness and peace.

After the rape, I struggled for a time to see myself as someone with the power and autonomy to say "no" or to say "yes"—to see myself as someone with the freedom to choose. Only a month after the rape, a man I had been dating pressured me to have sex and I gave in, even though neither my body nor my spirit was ready. I hid my tears from him in the dark and threw up afterward. It was over a year after the rape before I said "no" to sex. I was afraid of what would happen if I said "no," and I believed that I had lost my right to say "no." Because my *no* had been so profoundly ignored, I didn't think I had one anymore, and when there is no *no*, there cannot really be a freely chosen *yes*. I felt as though a woman whose body had been used as mine had been used was not a woman who had the right to say "no" to anyone. Then, one day, when I could only see emptiness in my eyes in the mirror, I decided to search for myself—to find that person I had been before the rape. I found her at the bottom of the emptiness, buried underneath the rape. She was holding hands with my power to decide what I would do and who I would be. She was so very glad to see me. If you have lost your sense of power, know that it is not gone, but only buried, waiting for you to reclaim it. Choose to possess yourself again.

One cannot choose to be raped. But one can choose to survive.

After the rape, we are waiting, many strong, at the edge of the cave, in that space between light and dark, to meet you, to hear your stories, to acknowledge your truths, to stand beside you as you seek justice, to raise our arms in protest with you, and to remind you—as you will remind us—that love and beauty, like hope, cannot be stolen. We're shining the light. Can you see it?

annu saini

LETTER TO MY RAPIST

    I feel sorry for you
because you did not kill me
There was a point when
you were holding my neck and
a kind spirit in me
almost whispered
Do it
Snap it
Right through
the throat
One Way
the only way
to stop the truth
from stalking you
Right through
The throat
Snap it
Killing the wind
that almost

    whispered to you
But didn't
And now it's that
kind spirit
—what you thought was a

kind spirit——that
Laughs
at your naivety
in sparing me

    Because you
let me live and
that was a big mistake
The truth is fierce and
the silence
of that breath
was the biggest
is the only
Lie
I ever told.

Sara Durnan

PARA TODO LO QUE SE MARCHO

Ella quiere que su voz regrese
La ha perdido hace un año, nueve meses y
veinticinco días
Se le iba con los brazos poderosos
Se le iba con el apreton sofocante
Se le iba con los oídos que jugaban a ser sordos
Se le iba cuando las violentas manos reclamaban su
piel
Era el momento en que se dió cuenta de que la
palabra "no" era inútil

Ella pide que sus lágrimas se sequen
Han persistido desde hace un año, nueve meses y
veinticinco días
Han caído por el horror que es recordarlo
Han caído por la muerte de su alma
Han caído por su deseo de ahogarse
Han caído porque no ha podido acallar las
pesadillas
Todavía están cayendo porque él respira
profundamente y la vida de él continua como si
nada hubiera pasado

Ella espera que su fuerza vuelva
La necesita desde hace un año, nueve meses y

veinticinco días

Con su fuerza romperá el silencio

Con su fuerza recordará que su vida vale la pena

Con su fuerza respirará profundamente

Con su fuerza, su vida continuará

Jamás será como si nada hubiera pasado, pero si
se abandona a si misma, será como si él hubiera
tomado todo de ella

FOR ALL THAT LEFT HER

She wants her voice to return
It has been lost for one year, nine months, and
twenty-five days
It left with his powerful arms
It left with his suffocating grip
It left with his ears that played deaf
It left when his violent hands demanded her skin
It was the moment in which she realized that the
word *no* was useless

She begs her tears to dry up
They have persisted for one year, nine months, and
twenty-five days
They have fallen for the horror that is remembering
They have fallen for the death of her soul
They have fallen for her desire to drown herself
They have fallen because she could not silence the
nightmares
They are still falling because he breathes deeply
and his life continues as if nothing
happened

She hopes her strength will return
She has needed it for one year, nine months, and
twenty-five days

With her strength she will shatter the silence
With her strength she will remember that her life is
worth it
With her strength she will breathe deeply
With her strength her life will continue
It will never be as if nothing had happened, but if
she gives up on herself,
it will be as if he had taken all of her

Harriet Jay

ANOTHER POST ABOUT RAPE

*This piece was originally published
on the blog* Fugitivus *and has been
reprinted with permission.*

I consistently use that title because I mean for it to
operate as a trigger warning. I write a lot about rape,
but sometimes I write about other things, and I don't
want anybody to be taken off guard, transitioning from
"help computer" into "WTF rape-talk." In case you
were wondering.

I was re-reading my five billion goddamn posts
about rape and force, and I realized that (surprise!)
there is a more succinct way for me to express what I
am thinking. I tend to go on and on, circling a subject,
trying to get out everything in my head that possibly
relates to it, and then sometimes find that I never really addressed the subject at all. So, here is what I
wanted to say in those five billion posts about rape:

Women are raised being told by parents, teachers,
media, peers, and all surrounding social strata that

- it is not okay to set solid and distinct boundaries and reinforce them immediately and
  dramatically when crossed ("mean bitch")

- it is not okay to appear distraught or emotional ("crazy bitch")

- it is not okay to make personal decisions that the adults or peers in your life do not agree with, and it is not okay to refuse to explain those decisions to others ("stuck-up bitch")

- it is not okay to refuse to agree with somebody, over and over and over again ("angry bitch")

- it is not okay to have (or express) conflicted, fluid, or experimental feelings about yourself, your body, your sexuality, your desires, and your needs ("bitch got daddy issues")

- it is not okay to use your physical strength (if you have it) to set physical boundaries ("dyke bitch")

- it is not okay to raise your voice ("shrill bitch")

- it is not okay to completely and utterly shut down somebody who obviously likes you ("mean dyke/frigid bitch")

If we teach women that there are only certain ways they may acceptably behave, then we should not be surprised when they behave in those ways. And we should not be surprised when they behave in these ways during attempted or completed rapes.

Women who are taught not to speak up too loudly or too forcefully or too adamantly or too demandingly are not going to shout *no* at the top of their goddamn lungs just because some guy is getting uncomfortably close. Women who are taught not to keep arguing are not going to *keep* saying *no.*

Women who are taught that their needs and desires are not to be trusted, that they are fickle and wrong and are not to be interpreted by the woman herself, are not going to know how to argue with "but you liked kissing, I just thought…"

Women who are taught that physical confrontations make them look crazy will not start hitting, kicking, and screaming until it's too late, if they do at all.

Women who are taught that a display of their emotional state will have them labeled hysterical and crazy (which is how their perception of events will be discounted) will not be willing to run from a room disheveled and screaming and crying.

Women who are taught that certain established boundaries are frowned upon as too rigid and unnecessary are going to find themselves in situations that move further faster, before they realize that their first impression was right and that they are in a dangerous room with a dangerous person.

Women who are taught that refusing to flirt back results in an immediately hostile environment will continue to unwillingly and unhappily flirt with somebody who is invading their space and giving them creep alerts.

People wonder why women don't "fight back," but they don't wonder about it when women back down in arguments, are interrupted, purposefully lower and modulate their voices to express less emotion, make obvious signals that they are uninterested in conversation or close physical proximity and are ignored.

They don't wonder about all those daily social interactions in which women are quieter, ignored, or invisible, because those social interactions seem normal. They seem normal to women, and they seem normal to men, because we were all raised in the same cultural pond, drinking the same Kool-Aid.

And then, all of a sudden, when women are raped, all these natural and invisible social interactions become evidence that the woman wasn't truly raped. Because she didn't fight back, or yell loudly, or run, or kick, or punch. She let him into her room when it was obvious what he wanted. She flirted with him, she kissed him. She stopped saying no, after a while. These rules for social interactions that women are taught to obey are more than grease for the patriarchy wheel. Women are taught both that these rules will protect them and that disobeying these rules will result in punishment.

Here's a situation every woman is familiar with: Some guy she knows—perhaps a casual acquaintance, perhaps just some dude at the bus stop—is obviously infatuated with her. He's making conversation, he's giving her the eye. She doesn't like him. She doesn't want to talk to him. She doesn't want him near her. He is freaking her out. She could disobey the rules and tell him to *get the fuck away from her* and continue screaming *get the fuck away from me* every time he tries to step closer or speak to her again. And then he will be all, "I was just talking to you! WTF!" and everybody else will be all, "Yeah, seriously, why'd you freak out at a guy just talking to you?" and refuse to offer the support she needs to be safe from the dude. Or, the guy might become hostile, violent even. Ladies, you've seen that look: the "bitch can't ignore me" look. It's a source of constant confusion, from the moment when you start budding breasts to just a moment ago, when that man who just told you how pretty you are is now calling you a stupid ugly whore, all because you didn't get in his car.

OR

You could follow the rules. You could flirt back a little, look meek, not talk, not move away. You might have to put up with a lot more talking, you might have to put up with him trying to ask you out to lunch every day, or you might even have to go out to lunch with him. You might have to deal with him copping a feel. But he won't turn violent on you, and neither will the spectators who have watched him browbeat you into a frightened and flirtatious corner.

So we learn the rules will protect us. We learn that, when we step out of line, somebody around us might very well turn crazy. Might hurt us. And we won't be defended by onlookers, who think we've provoked the craziness somehow. So, having your ass grabbed at the bus stop, having to go out to dinner with a guy you fucking can't stand, maybe even having to fuck him once or twice—it's a small sacrifice to avoid being ostracized, insulted, verbally abused, and possibly physically assaulted.

It's a rude awakening when a woman gets raped and follows the rules she has been taught her whole life—doesn't refuse to talk, doesn't refuse to flirt, doesn't walk away ignoring him, doesn't hit, doesn't scream, doesn't fight, doesn't raise her voice, doesn't deny she liked kissing—and finds out afterward that she is now to blame for the rape. *She followed the rules.* The rules that were supposed to *keep the rape from happening*. The rules that would keep her from being fair game for verbal and physical abuse. *Breaking* the rules, rather than following them, is supposed to result in punishment. For every time she lowered her voice, let go of a boundary, didn't move away, let her needs be conveniently misinterpreted, and was given positive reinforcement and a place in society, she is now being told that all that was wrong, this one time, and *she should have known that*—duh.

For anybody who has ever watched the gendered social interactions of women—watched a woman get browbeaten into accepting attention she doesn't want, watched a woman get interrupted while speaking, watched a woman deny she is upset about being insulted in public, watched a woman get grabbed because of what she was wearing, watched a woman stop arguing—and said and done nothing, you never have the right to ever ask, "Why didn't she fight back?"

She didn't fight back because you told her not to. Ever. *Ever. You told her that was okay, and necessary, and right.* You didn't give her an alternative. You didn't say, "Unless…" You said, "Good for you, shutting up and backing down 99 percent of the time."

Nobody obtains the superpower to behave dramatically differently during a frightening confrontation. Women will behave the same way they have been taught to behave in all social, professional, and sexual interactions. And they will be pretty goddamned surprised to come out the other end and find out that means they can legally be raped at any time, by just about anybody.

I am focusing on women here. I tend to do that, being one and all, but let's mention something about men. If men have been raised to behave aggressively, to discount what women and weaker men want and feel and say, to obtain power and social standing through force, to deny that emotions exist, to feel that women are fundamentally a different species, to set a boundary and keep it *no matter what*, to make a decision and stick to it *no matter what*, to feel entitled to sex, to feel they will be ostracized and possibly physically attacked if they don't acquire sex with women, to feel under threat of harassment and attack if they don't constantly maintain a hyper-masculine exterior, to prove their manhood through dangerous and degrading physical activities…

…if you have seen men behave in this way, and encouraged it, and thought it was normal, so normal that you didn't even see it…then you never have the right to say, "He couldn't possibly have done that," when you hear that your brother raped somebody.

That wasn't concise at all. What I mean to say is this:

The way that men and women interact on a daily basis is the way they interact when rape occurs. The social dynamics we see at play between men and women are the same social dynamics that cause men to feel that rape is okay and women to feel that they have no right to object. And if you accept those social interactions as normal and appropriate in your day-to-day life, then there is absolutely no reason you should be shocked that rape occurs without screaming, without fighting, without bruising, without provocation, and without prosecution. Behavior exists on a continuum. Rape doesn't inhabit its own little corner of the world where everything is suddenly all different now. The behavior you accept today is the behavior that becomes rape tomorrow. And you very well might accept it then, too.

Mia Mingus

TRANSFORMATIVE AND DISABILITY JUSTICE

I don't know very much about healing. I know about survival and how to make it through the night—each minute alive, a cowardly victory. I know about shame; I know about fear.

I know about resiliency. I know about joy. I know about getting lost in a song, about the way the morning ocean air feels on my skin at sunrise; the way the sweeping fields turn from blues to purples to greens as the day awakens. I know about love.

I know about longing. The echo of a heartbeat. The feeling of never knowing home, and the naive ache that someday you might finally know. The moment you realize that some decisions are forever and cannot be changed or made right. I know heartbreak. I know about loss.

But healing I do not know very much about. I believe that healing is possible and though I may not understand its magic or those who wield it, I work for it. Every day.

I did not come to this work, the work of transformative and disability justice, to be healed. I came to transformative justice because it was the only framework I found that could hold the complexities of intimate and state violence, accountability and healing, and systemic and personal transformation. I wanted something more than just responding to the impacts and consequences of violence without addressing the root causes. I wanted something more connected to the material reality of violence than the traditional "prevention" strategies out there, which are largely based in education and policy that pushes for more criminalization and heavier sentencing. Campaigns urge survivors to report their abuse, but that is simply not an option for so many of us whose communities already experience daily violence from the state, or who would likely experience more violence, shame, and isolation from our families and communities. It was the only way forward for a queer disabled Korean woman transracial and transnational adoptee survivor.

I came to disability justice because it was one of the only places where all of me could be seen. It was a place to be able to breathe, a place to find language for the silence, a place to break isolation with connection. There was no other place to hold disability as political and in connection with other systems of oppression and violence. In all of my time in activist and movement spaces, I rarely, if ever, heard anyone talk about disability, accessibility, ableism, freakery, or able-bodied supremacy. My disability informed my entire life and all of who I was; it was a huge part of my experience as a queer woman of color adoptee and organizer; it was not just an "add-on" or individual problem. Disability justice became the place where I could understand and explain the deep connections between able-bodied supremacy, white supremacy, and capitalism. It was a way to make sense and communicate things that I didn't have language for before, things that were so incredibly isolating and painful. Disability justice has saved my life more times than I can say.

I grew up on a small rural island in the Caribbean. Transnationally and transracially adopted at six months, I arrived there as a disabled baby, needing immediate and serious medical care and attention. Like many disabled children, the medical industrial complex was a huge part of my childhood. I wore a brace from the time I can remember and my foot, leg, back, and walk were under heavy examination. I had surgeries on my leg and my ear, sometimes on both at the same time. I had severe ear infections as a child and can remember regular hearing tests, ear drops, ear plugs, and holding absolutely still as my ear was being examined. Hospitals, physical therapists, healers, brace makers, doctors, nurses, and surgeries were the norm. They shaped how I saw myself and the way that I learned to understand my body, as something to be fixed, something that wasn't "mine," and a place where consent didn't exist.

I was adopted from Korea when I was six months old by two white, middle-class, married parents. That same year, my mother, along with nine other women founded an organization to help victims of domestic violence, rape, and sexual assault. I grew up in a close-knit, politicized, multi-racial, second-wave feminist community. As I grew, so did the organization; children and community constantly surrounded us.

Growing up, I understood intimate violence to be something that was not just happening to my friends and the people I knew, but something that was happening everywhere. My mother's organization was constantly at capacity, responding to the survivors and families in crisis that had nowhere to go and needed help. They saw woman after woman, day in and day out, and visited the hospital night after night. I understood the pervasiveness of violence and was taught how to identify it.

We marched in Take Back the Night marches, discussed racism around the dinner table, and wore shirts to the organization's annual women's race that said,"You can't beat a woman." And yet, through all of this, no one ever connected the violence I was experiencing in the medical industrial complex to the work that the organization was doing to end violence against women and children. No one ever saw the medical industrial complex, in and of itself—let alone the sexual abuse I experienced inside of it—as violent and traumatic.

When I talk about surviving the violence of the medical industrial complex, I mean the actual cutting into my flesh, the literal invasion of my body, the examining by all kinds of hands and instruments. I mean the public stripping in front of groups of male and white doctors. I mean the "be a good patient," "grateful adoptee," "obedient girl" suffocating cage I was expected to live in. I mean the conversations that were had about me but never with me—the decisions that got made about my body that I had no say in, that I did not consent to. I mean the white, imperialist, able-bodied supremacy of whose bodies get valued and whose get coded as disposable or needing to be fixed or saved. I mean the sexual abuse that is considered regular practice and the incidents of sexual abuse that are gross abuses of power. I mean the way doctors would treat me, as if I were theirs to mold and shape, as if I should want a non-disabled body, as if they knew me better than I knew myself.

The violence of adoption normalized the violence I would experience in the medical industrial complex and beyond. Transnational adoption of children of color and the medical treatment of disabled people are so normalized as obvious, sensible solutions, with people rarely, if ever, talking to the ones most impacted: adoptees and disabled people. We are people to be saved—sad, tragic stories people tell. We are the unwanteds and the undesirables. We are spectacles of novelty and pity. We should be grateful someone cares enough about us to give us a chance to live, even if that means the erasure and silencing of our bodies and our legacies.

I often wonder if my white adoptive parents had any idea what it meant to hand the body of a tiny disabled Korean adoptee girl over to a white, male-dominated, ableist medical establishment whose history is one of experimentation, colonization, eugenics, and population control.

This is how I came to transformative justice, in my mid-twenties, as a closeted survivor of child sexual abuse from the medical industrial complex, from the state, and a young organizer working for the liberation of my communities. I already knew the immense levels of violence enacted by the state, and I knew that I, like many others, did not look to state systems to keep me safe because they had been the sites of my abuse. I wanted something more than criminalization, punishment, and trauma, as I saw the harmful impacts of the police and prison system on my communities. I learned from radical women of color how the state and intimate violence were deeply connected, and I witnessed how the state mimicked the tactics of the most cunning abuser. I learned through working with the Breaking the Silence Project, generationFIVE, and the Atlanta Transformative Justice Collaborative that child sexual abuse is not just a form of intimate violence, but it has also been used by the state as a tool of colonization, slavery, war, and oppression—that disabled children and adults are twice as likely to be victims of sexual violence and abuse.[1]

At its most basic, transformative justice is about responding to violence in ways that don't cause more harm. It is community-based responses to violence that don't collude with state (prisons, police, the criminal legal system, etc.), communal (vigilantism, public shaming, etc.), or systemic (racism, sexism, etc.) violence. Transformative justice seeks individual and collective justice for the people and communities impacted; personal and political transformation; and response and prevention of the violence that occurred.

I have been involved in transformative justice and child sexual abuse work, specifically creating transformative justice responses to child sexual abuse, for the past eight years, and in that time I have been part of a small current of folks across the country working to build our capacity and prepare for what a transformative justice response to an incident of child sexual abuse would actually look like. I have been part of responses to violence that have used a transformative justice framework to respond in a way that not only meets immediate needs of safety, but also works to secure longer-term goals such as accountability and prevention. Many of these attempts have been huge

---

1 generationFIVE, *Toward Transformative Justice: A Liberatory Approach to Child Sexual Abuse and Other Forms of Intimate and Community Violence*, 2007.

places of learning for all involved about how much we need and simply don't have yet: individual and communal healing skills, experience and knowledge about accountability processes, the years or decades needed to not just hold someone accountable but to work for their transformation. I have been lucky enough to live in this historical moment when transformative justice and community accountability have become much more visible and are widely being learned about and tried. The historical moment we are in feels like a moment of experimentation, and most of us who are engaging in community accountability or transformative justice are learning far more from what we didn't do well or wish we had done better, than we are fully executing transformative justice or community accountability. We are trying out strategies, then tweaking them and trying again, and sharing what we learn with each other as much as possible.

Many of us envision the kind of coordinated community capacity that could hold healing circles and develop safety plans for survivors; work to build deeper emotional capacity and educate community members so that they can confidently intervene in instances of violence and support each other to do so; and train folks in accountability processes and healing for people who have caused harm or perpetuated violence, who oftentimes have been victims of violence themselves. We envision responses that can hold the more complex and blurry parts of intimate violence that are messy and challenging. For example, not just the healing and safety of survivors, but also accountability, knowing the very real history we have of responses to violence that have resulted in harmful legislation and criminalization. Case in point, the sex offender registry has not lessened sexual violence, but instead criminalized more and more people (many of whom are not "sex offenders") and funneled them into a prison system that is not built to encourage accountability nor transformation. Another complex and blurry part of intimate violence that is hard for most people to sit with is the humanization of offenders and the very real and complicated relationships that exist between survivors and the people who have harmed us that are not always as black and white as we've been told. It is not always as easy as "good" or "bad," and for so many of us our experiences of abuse are tied up with dependence, love, desire, survival, affection, and care. We envision responses that are generative and challenge all of us to examine and be accountable for the very real ways that we have all caused harm or been complicit in violence.

If I do know anything about healing, I know that my work around disability justice, transformative justice, and child sexual abuse has been hugely healing. I have been longing for disability- and transformative justice my entire life. My work around disability justice is what I wished I had growing up and when I was coming into political consciousness. I know that currently, accountability from the people who violated me is not possible, like so many others who have survived violence at the hands of the state, and I know it won't be possible until we can get concrete responses to violence on the ground in our communities. I know we won't be able to hold the state accountable until we can learn to hold ourselves accountable and until we can grow full, vibrant communities that are skilled in genuine accountability and true transformative work. As a survivor of sexual violence, it can feel overwhelming once you begin to comprehend the enormous prevalence and impact of sexual violence. It can leave you feeling hopeless. Working to build transformative-justice responses to child sexual abuse has been inspiring—nourishing, even—because it is a concrete beginning to ending child sexual abuse, and sexual violence at large.

I don't know how to separate my activism from my healing. They are one in the same. Every day, I work in honor of those who have come before me, with deep gratitude for those working with me and in service of those who will come after me.

Transformative justice is not easy, but I believe that it is the only way toward a world where sexual violence doesn't exist. At the crux of transformative justice, we are saying that no one is disposable and that healing and transformation for all of us is possible. We are saying that intimate violence is so pervasive, and violence is so systematic, that to lock up everyone who has ever harmed someone would be to lock up most of us. We are saying that for most of us, our relationships with the people who have harmed us are complicated and not always as simple as "good" or "bad." We are saying that no one is born knowing how to sexually abuse children, how to rape, how to torture, those things are learned.

I am not a healer, but I am an organizer, a community builder, and an evidence-leaver for those coming after me. As a survivor of violence, I do not wish violence on anyone, even those who have perpetrated violence. Nor do I wish more trauma, terror, or shame to those who have caused trauma, terror, or shame. I know that it is not the way to liberation—I feel it in my bones, my spirit, and my soul.

I do not wish anyone any more haunted, sleepless nights.

I hold hope for my own healing and transformation and for yours. For all of us, I pray for peaceful nights and purpose in the face of hopelessness. And I work for something powerful enough to transform ourselves, each other, and the systems we live in, yet accessible enough to be held in even the tiniest of hands.

Leah Lakshmi Piepzna-Samarasinha &
kyisha williams

BADASS RESILIENCE BLACK AND BROWN
FEMME SURVIVOR AFFIRMATIONS

*These affirmations were taken from a
collective keynote delivered by Leah
Lakshmi Piepzna-Samarasinha and
Kyisha Williams for a Planned Parenthood
conference, in Toronto in March 2012, on
queer women's sexual desire and danger.*

I recognize and celebrate the Love I encounter every day.

I love myself unconditionally (no matter what).

I do not hurt myself, or act in ways that contribute to my self-destruction; the self-destruction the world wants me to take part in. I also do not act in ways that are destructive to my community, because we are interdependent.

I have the power to heal, by myself and collectively, the trauma my body and spirit hold due to abuse and oppression.

I attract only healthy relationships.

All my relationships are loving and harmonious (including the one with self).

I release any desperation and allow love to find me.

I have the power to have my heart's desire.

If I can figure out what I want, I can figure out how to get it.

I make a beautiful life for myself out of my heart's desires.

My body is a site of pleasure and power.

I understand that I am connected to All (everything).

I am a being whose home is among the stars; I am brilliant and full of light (darkness).

There is never anything to worry about.

I focus on my power, not my powerlessness.

I trust myself.

And when I believe and trust in myself, so do others.

I express my needs and feelings despite fear.

I embrace the velocity of change.

I trust in the process of life.

I am at peace.

I get to be surprised.

I get to make a new story.

LETTER 15: SPECIAL

Dear Sister,

I never wanted to be special again. You, me, we been "special."

I remember special: pulling down my skirts, pulling up turtlenecks. Liking huge-ass boy pants. Eating till you vomited, hoping special would go away. Then starving till you passed out in hopes you would go away instead.

And no one understands why such a pretty girl would...

never date

eat so much

never get out of bed

hate the doctor so much

sleep around

wear such clothing

cut that pretty hair

cut that pretty skin

Trying to find the special that fits.

I tried to be a "different special," and then remembered that being special invites the eyes, the probing, the intrusiveness.

Who wants more of that special?

And it's hard, no? Because in a world where everyone wants to be special, where the only way you get to be worthy is special, how, then, do you talk about special when it clogs till you can't breathe?

Ain't that what they mean? When they want to tell us: "you're not worthy."

"You ain't special!"

And for you and me, how you wish they weren't wrong about special and how you wish they weren't right about what they mean. That you're not worth the good attention, the bad attention, the screaming, the grabbing for your "good hair," "thick thighs."

I know you know special.

But, it's not about special, it's not about taking back the night, or power, or monologues, or movements, or the thousands of things and ways that you are told to "fix" yourself, as if you were broken before.

I want you to remember you.

It's about remembering you don't have to be special.

There is no judge and jury that should live in your mind and especially not your heart, telling you the right way to be.

It's about the world outside the word, that said it would make us special, bend and form it to its will just to be worthy.

It's about the first time I remembered my *NO* mattered. About forgetting and remembering thousands of times, again and again.

The way things happened to us makes us feel the world wants us to forget that we are enough
and this is how I remember
over and over again
I write to you
I talk to you

and there is no special there.

Here.

There needs to be a new wor(l)d for us. A whole new word; one that doesn't make us jump or cry or shake in the night.

One that holds us close as we work through it.

Not special, that picked us for terrors and questions and the coping and the fear;

not special, tucked into our bellies, under our skins, into our scars, under a silence that makes "special girls" forget the words they could be before and the worlds they can make after

a whole new wor(l)d that loves us

the way we are meant to love ourselves

whomever we are and need to be.

Love You,
Sydette/BA/Whatever I need to be today

Radical Companionship

Alexis Pauline Gumbs

&

& on the way to the store & on the stop for the
mail & before the first outfit & after the last change
& under the spirals in your notebook & above the
water spot in the ceiling & when you look down at
your shoes & and on the run away & in the line for
whatever & for three cups of tea & in the bathroom
mirror & before & after & when you don't want to
talk & when you do want to talk & when you can't
listen anymore & when you play the song fifty times
& when you almost knock on the door & and when
you whisper "why" & when you feed the pain &
when you starve the silence & when you turn off the
phone & when you repaint the walls of your hiding
place & when you climb trees to scream your own
name & when you try to explain & when you let
them assume & when you make your favorite meal
& can't even eat it & in the blank space after the
words "I know" & in the opening before regret &
when even the tears don't flow right & when you're
too dehydrated to cry & when you're dizzy from
drinking water for days & nothing has washed away
& when you want to try again & when you avoid
yourself & when you ignore everyone else & today
& yesterday & tomorrow & when you open the
book & when you throw it at your reflection & with

the kids in the car & with the boss on the phone
& on the day of the first memory & on the nights
awake & when the wind feels excellent & when
rain won't end & when even one star would change
something & when darkness is a cloak & when you
need a new toothbrush & when you don't know
how you got there & when the vegetables come up
& when the birds sound crazy & when your clothes
don't fit & when snow looks like the world ending
& when anything could melt you & when you are in
love & when the first cut is the deepest & when the
last straw is looking you in the eye & when the light
bill is due & when the Internet won't work & when
someone has your same shoes & when you must be
on the wrong planet & when you go home early &
you make up errands so you don't have to be there
& and on that national holiday that you completely
forgot & at the concert & all the poetry sounds the
same & and when the glass frames in photography
galleries are an excuse to look at yourself more criti-
cally than ever & when nobody knows your name
& when your business is in the street & you notice
that your friendships are strategies for avoiding
yourself & when you don't trust anybody anymore &
and when dance class is canceled & when you start
to feel the rhythm of your own walk again & when
your socks don't match & when you stop caring &
when when when & when & when & when it feels
right & when it feels like hell & when you wish you
hadn't worn eyeliner & when no one can even tell
you are screaming & when figure skating comes on
& when the power goes out & the fireworks outside
might be gunshots & when even the crickets are
holding back & in the meetings & when you just

might be okay & over the sidewalk chalk & when you are so grateful for the sun & between the lines & when the GPS leads you into a dead end & when just want to keep driving & when you can't find your keys & you pat yourself on the back for hiding it all so well & when you just listen to the acoustic guitar Pandora station all day and cry & when the bass drowns everything out & when you remember & when you forget & between here & wherever from now to forever **it's you & me & we are not alone.**

Love,
Lex

LETTER 16: LIGHT

Dear Sister,

I hope by the time this letter reaches you, you are well. I hope you can sleep at night and no longer cringe if someone tries to touch you. I hope you realize that it wasn't your fault. If you fought and got hurt like I did, I hope you're not angry at the wisdom that told you to do that. And if you decided not fight but still got hurt, I hope you're not mad at the wisdom that told you not to fight.

I hope you're not trying to be perfect all the time in an attempt to prove that you didn't deserve what happened to you. I hope you're not doing the worst things imaginable to prove that you don't care or telling yourself that since you feel like shit now you might as well act like shit.

I'm sorry, my sister. While the road you're on now will be long and difficult, know that you have company. You've been to hell, and worse yet, hell is inside you, and you need to reach for heaven every day to get back in balance. Let in those who want to help you, but close the door on those who help you dig deeper into a pit. At first it might be hard to distinguish between the two when everything feels like fear, but with time, you'll be able to tell the difference. Those who thought this would break you will see your truth in how you relight your core and grow bright and warm again.

Give yourself as much time as you need. Take forever if that's what it takes. Nothing is more important than your light. So take your time, sister. Go deep and stay in the dark as long as you need to feel safe again. Know that when you're ready to climb out of your hole, all of those who have been down there will be waiting for you here, in the light.

With light and love,
Your sister,
Shala

LETTER 17: A SAD SONG NO MORE

Dear Sister,

I used to know a sad song. A song that drew tears, stomach pains, and weak knees. A song that was the soundtrack to every unwanted entrance he made into my precious body. A song that got louder with every lash, bruise, and physical reminder of him. A song that sometimes sedated me into a deep sleep so my brain could not remember anymore.

He is no more, ever since the day I got the courage to tell my mother what he did to me. That winter day, on the phone, hearing my mother's tears and anger was the first time I really knew that my mother loved me. Beyond any question or doubt, my mother loved me. I was her baby, a feeling that I was unsure of until that point.

My courage was prompted by Women's Studies courses. I always knew that what happened was wrong, but some of the information in my class made me feel empowered to expose and embrace my experience.

From this I know the following:

I am not broken. No one needs to make it their task to fix me. I am who I am in spite, because, and regardless of the girl-turned-woman that my mother's brother tried to break. My spirit and body can, did, and will continue to endure.

It wasn't my fault. I can spend time trying to figure out all of the things I could have done differently, but at the end of every road, he had a bigger choice to make, and he did.

I am still standing. I am not weak. These legs, this body, this spirit is strong.

I will not sing my sad song anymore. The sound and lyrics are memories. I refuse to give that sad song the power to drown me any longer. I am new each day, so each day I know a new song. I will never sing myself to sleep to his song again.

You, sister, if you have a sad song, I encourage you to sing it no more—that song is not worthy of the beauty and essence of your life. Your days are worthy of resounding joy, laughter, and a soundtrack reflecting that.

Be encouraged,
Desire

Allison McCarthy

THE PEARL

What does it mean to be pure—to feel pure—after sexual assault and rape? Before the rape, I had my Christian definition of purity, which (for my denomination) meant no dating outside of the religion and no sex before marriage. But, really, I can't speak about sexual purity without talking about Tía Nikki and the pearl.

I can tell you that the concept of sexual purity usually means very little to an eleven-year-old, but I learned about young women and their "pearls" as my great aunt helped me into my coat and hat one winter evening after a leisurely family dinner. It was the kind of family gathering where my cousins and I spent the majority of the evening playing with each other's toys and watching cartoons in the basement, while the grown-ups drank coffee and talked among themselves around the dining room table.

As one of the three "little ones," I wasn't used to being singled out for my aunt's attention, but as she smoothed a brown wool cap over my hair, she brushed my bangs over to the side of my forehead and held my face between her hands. "Ay, *princesa*, you are going to have such a beautiful pearl."

Thinking her words were literal and that a special gift was forthcoming, I asked Tía Nikki where my new pearls were, but she only smiled and clasped my hands. "The pearl grows inside of a virtuous girl who will someday—not long from now but very soon, *mi hijita*—be a woman." I was growing up. I was still pure. "Promise me you'll guard the pearl carefully," she said. I swore that I would. She patted my head affectionately and said that I was a precious gem, lovely and beautiful to behold. I believed every word.

The emphasis on my chastity, my purity of thought and deed, was meant to protect me from unwanted pregnancy or disease, possibly even from the heartbreak of youth's passion. After all, a pearl is the product of irritability: a hard, crystallized bit of dirt and sand formed into an iridescent jewel within the soft tissue of a living shell. My pearl was innocence of mind and body; someday long in the future, I assumed, I would exchange my innocent pearl for adult knowledge—marriage, intimacy, love, and commitment. A woman could mature and then choose those things freely. A woman would have time and support in making those choices.

But after the rape, I found that whatever pearl I had imagined no longer existed inside of me. After all, I was no longer innocent. What had I chosen? Nothing. Certainly not the secrecy or the shame. Trapped in the limited confines of my mind, I forced myself to stand trial for my rapist's crimes. I convinced myself that his evil intentions were my own, that I had caused the assaults to happen, and that my punishment was an eternal shame and private burden to bear.

After the rape, I lost my faith in any innocence that I had once known. There was no one to trust, no place of understanding. The pearl I had once envisioned—tucked away in safety, prized and glowing—was gone.

Only grit remained in its place.

I had survived, and although the pearl was gone before I had a chance to claim it for myself, as it turned out, the grit did more for me than the pearl ever could. The grit I felt within me as I endured state-sponsored counseling, social workers, and the endless legal procession was tangible, solid, and at times, the only real comfort I could find when faced with the judgments of outsiders. It wasn't soft or shiny; I could not yet lay my head down to rest on it or relax enough to let anyone else see it, but I could hold onto that grit when everything in my life seemed to exist in a free fall of loss and despair. I could turn that bit of grit between my fingers, turn it over in my hands, and wait for it to change into something else.

Over time, I found that the grit sustained me, and gradually I realized that for me, the grit far outweighs the value of any pearl. In theory, the pearl would have eventually been given away, but the grit of a survivor is a different kind of innocence, one that cannot be traded, bartered, or stolen. As survivors, we often feel compromised in the most fundamental of ways. I needed to exonerate myself of any lingering guilt in order to realize that it was never my wrongdoing or my shame to bear—it was my rapist's. That grit is my reclaimed innocence.

You are still valued and you are still here.

In the journey of healing, I hope there is grit along your road as you struggle to endure the worst. That grit is the solace of self—the purest bit of love and belief that you will ever hold. It is there for you to claim in your own time and can never ever be taken away. Your grit as a woman and a survivor is far more precious, cherished, and essential to the life force.

Sister, I cannot offer you pearls or easy comfort, but I can share that the grit that emerges from these dark hours is the faith that will tether you to your true self.

LETTER 18: AN HOURLY RECKONING

Dear Sister,

Surviving is the process of living and dying each day. A primordial balancing. The ability to walk through level-five earthquakes. When you feel the impossible breathing down your neck, you are on the right path. As long as you continue moving— whether you crawl, wander, or run—your energy will keep you alive.

As kids, my siblings and I would get in trouble if we were sick, so I always was. When we could afford to, we would go to the doctor. He would never find anything wrong but ask why such a young child was so stressed. "Is everything alright at home?" he would question, although my father was in the room. I would glance in his direction but remain silent, frozen, and nod my head in consent.

It is easier for me to believe that something is wrong if I am showing external symptoms. Being sick gave me a sense of power over a mind, which would hide itself for days and seemed to be beyond my control. I would plummet into depressions that I did not understand. Depressions so deep that when

I learned to drive I would end up at my destina
tion with no memory of the drive itself. And since I
didn't learn about the concept of dissociation until
I went to college, when I developed rheumatoid ar-
thritis at seventeen, it gave me the perfect excuse to
ignore myself and delve further and further into the
grind of daily knee, hip, and knuckle deterioration.

I only walk you through all this so that when a
migraine develops, you look inside. If a cold turns
into a chronic cough and lasts for months, take a day
to yourself. If a morning comes when it hurts too
much to get out of bed, come back into your body
and choose to live.

We are restricted in this society. We can't steer
through life without nicking our props on the reefs
of misogyny, running around on the sandbars of self-
doubt. The fish are gone, there aren't enough odd jobs
to go around, and when we think we have found a
clear passage, the deadhead of identity knocks a hole
clear through the hull, sinking our boat.

Surviving is the process of finding new connections each day. An hourly reckoning. It's the ability
to trust even though it seems impossible to look
anyone in the eyes again. Sometimes we stumble
toward each other and find a community whose energy will keep us alive.

I love you,
Rebecca Wyllie de Echeverria

anna saini

AN UNLIKABLE SURVIVOR

Perhaps you are one of the magnanimous survivors who convert their trauma into acts of altruism, who exude goodness, who are contemporary saints. Or perhaps you are more like me. You have to make an effort to be likeable because much of the time you feel angry, sad, and embittered. You are this way because of what happened to you, but what happened to you does not dictate who you are. Who you are is a composite of all these features, likeable and un-likeable, that you've accumulated over a lifetime of trauma, triumph, and all the experiences in between.

No one has the right to judge you. We are survivors and we fuck up like anyone else. We have not gained some divine likability by virtue of being survivors. We are not all Mother Theresa trying to save the world one at a time. We are fucked up by virtue of being survivors; someone (many people, actually) fucked with me, and now I have this title that I never asked for—"survivor"—because I didn't die.

Perhaps if we met, you would be intimidated by me because I have publications, job titles, and academic letters after my name. But the truth is that I am a hot motherfucking mess. I blow up in meetings, I freak out on friends, and I sleep in to the point of irresponsibility. I've been fired from several jobs. As "survivors" it feels like we are expected to be these indecently kind people when we are more often high-maintenance and fractured. For all that I've been through, I find it is too much pressure to be a fully functioning human being.

I think it's fair to say that I have a hard time trusting people. I live on guard. I replay conversations and experiences and rake them for any indication of untrustworthiness. I consider motives ad nauseam. I periodically question my choices in friends, acquaintances, and colleagues. I investigate every seedling of doubt tirelessly. I maintain a high burden of proof. Eventually, I learn to put my fears to rest.

I must salve my own anxiety. As a survivor, I am part of a group suffering from post-traumatic stress disorder (PTSD). Survivors share this distinction with war veterans. I think this is because surviving is like fighting a war. There is no winner. All of us come out of it embattled, tough as shit, and we never receive a clear signal to stop fighting.

I also suffer from an autoimmune disorder related to PTSD. My nerves misfire pain responses that attack my insides as if they are foreign. The chasm between my mind and body is as puzzling to me as it is disconcerting. My body is fighting itself out of lack of recognition. I observe these bodily contradictions from a distance. I wind them into a concentrated unit that sits like a ball of yarn in my stomach. When I am bedridden by the early evening due to pain, that's when I return to the frustration living in my gullet, choking my digestion. My mind races on those evenings. I feel useless and lazy, gluttonous, amok with nerves.

I am angry at the unfairness of my condition. I am a veteran of an unnamed war. I have no home to return to, ravaged by conflict. I escaped with my life. It is not fair. There are so many who do not get out alive.

I refuse to act likable in the midst of all these demands. Likability is not a characteristic that is inherent to being a survivor. The only characteristic common among all survivors is that we have all overcome threats on our lives. And I, for one, believe that should be enough to ask of one person, especially myself.

Sumayyah Talibah

SISTER TO SISTER

sister
can you hear me
behind that wall of blue
that rose up
to block the pain
and ward off
the evil that men do?

sister
can you see me
waving my arms on the shore?

i have found a place
where you can rest
and lay those burdens down

come on
sister
we're almost there
can you feel
my hand in yours?
can you see the star
with its healing light
guiding us back home?

LETTER 19: I SEE YOU

Dear Sister,

I want you to know that I see you. I see your anger, your pain, your numbness. I see the war that has erupted between you and your body. You try to push the memories away, but they remain deeply rooted within your body. Your mind tries to disappear, leaving your body to fend for itself. But you are trapped; you can never truly escape. So there you lie, a casualty trapped inside a casualty.

No one else will ever understand the unique devastation that each of us feels. When the worst has happened. When you are absolutely overridden with guilt, doubt, and self-blame. The unrelenting drive of these feelings makes even a minute inside your own body excruciating. There is no way out, and there is no way back.

Whether we meet and recognize each other in this life or not, I see you. We are profoundly connected. I can never know the specificity of your pain, but we share an experience so deep and enduring that we can understand each other in a way unimaginable to others.

In the years after it happened to me, I felt like I was dying. Long after the perpetrators were gone, I experienced terror on a daily basis. Panic consumed my body, gripping my heart and lungs, overwhelming my consciousness. I was unable to eat, and as time went on I grew weaker and weaker. I felt myself fading. It was as if the perpetrators had taken root within me, distorting who I was until I could no longer distinguish myself from my injuries. Every ounce of my being was profoundly altered, and there was no way to know if I still existed underneath the symptoms. Surviving felt like an eternal battle, wearing away at my resolve, at everything I'd ever had.

Now, though I have many scars, some of which may rip open yet again, I have uncovered greater power and wisdom within myself than I knew was possible. That inner strength was cultivated by other survivors, my sisters-in-arms, who have listened to me, understood me, and given me love and compassion when I was unable to give any to myself. They have given me the safety to share things I thought I could never tell anyone, things that were driving me crazy when I was shouldering the burden of them alone. Most importantly, these women have been my spiritual companions. Our interconnectedness is a constant source of power, a blessing for which I am grateful every second of every day.

This connection that ties me to all other survivors keeps me sane when I cannot handle the world we live in. It feels awfully bizarre to intimately know the sickness that permeates so much of our seemingly enlightened society, the misogyny that allows so many people to stay silent while women are physically, sexually, emotionally, and spiritually violated.

We have witnessed the worst of humanity.

We must live with the knowledge that so many people, often accepted and admired in their communities, are capable of committing these atrocities. We are forced to face it, while others turn a blind eye. They don't want to see us. They would rather leave us to navigate the darkness alone and unarmed. But, Sister, you have millions of warrioresses who are eternally committed to you. We see you. You are greater, stronger, and much more enduring than the evil that has been done to you. You are infinitely valuable. And you are never alone.

As you continue your fight to survive and to heal, know that we are fighting with you. We will challenge those who allowed this to happen to you. We will walk with you, listen to you, support you, and offer you our unconditional acceptance. We are here—unwavering—as your comrades, as your defenders, as your sisters.

Amy Ernst

IN NORTH KIVU

An experience in North Kivu,
Democratic Republic of Congo

"There are two girls in the next room who were attacked by the soldiers who want to speak with you,"
says the hospital administrator in Isale village.

I walk into an expansive room with Maman Marie
Nzoli and Urbain at my side. Maman Marie is the
Director of COPERMA, a local Congolese organization. Urbain is one of Maman Marie's faithful em-
ployees and a friend. I've been working for a year with
COPERMA, identifying survivors of sexual violence.
I collect stories, memories of pain and terror, so that
we can better understand how to help each individual. The simple word "rape" simply can't convey a
person's needs. We speak to each survivor at length;
most haven't been to a hospital, some still have pain
in their abdomen, a few have had broken limbs, and
all say that they are afraid all the time. We use the
interviews to create a specific care plan and help each
individual's needs.

In the room there are several wooden benches and
a young girl sitting alone. Her eyes glance up at us
but drop immediately back to the ground and her

expression doesn't change. I don't need to ask if she is a survivor; I've seen this sad expression before.

I once thought that rape separates someone from their soul, but my mind changed when I saw her. This girl's face told me something else: rape takes a person further, not from their soul, but from their knowledge of their self-worth. It's difficult enough to believe that one is worthy of love, life, and joy. That knowledge is hard to hold on to, and rape makes it all the more impossible to grasp.

Every time I see a survivor with their eyes on the ground I want to say, "You're incredible! And beautiful throughout. You deserve love and comfort and laughter and hope, just like everyone else." I wish I could say, "You are worth everything beautiful in this world," and have her truly believe it.

I sit down on one of the benches across from this young girl and let Maman Marie take charge. The squat administrator man sits next to me and translates as Maman Marie and the girl speak in Kinande, the local language of the Nande people who live in this area.

Her name is Marcela. She says she doesn't know what the soldiers are doing here. One of the soldiers found her in the field. She was getting bananas to sell. It was one sole military. He spoke Swahili.

Marcela's eyes dart back and forth as if not knowing which spot on the floor to rest on.

She's afraid when she sees the soldiers.

"You must try to forget this," says Maman Marie in simple French.

Marcela responds, looking down at her feet now.

She says she'll never be able to forget it.

I wish I could speak Kinande and cut into the

conversation, "Please tell her it's necessary that she knows that this wasn't her fault, these were the actions of another person, and she didn't do anything wrong." Maman Marie translates for me.

I want to say so much more. I ask if she minds if I take a picture of her. If anything, it might cheer her up a little bit. She looks up with interest and nods her head yes. Her face doesn't change its sad expression and she still doesn't seem to know what to do with her eyes. I smile as big as I can and point to my teeth.

Smile with your teeth!

She laughs and smiles and she's beautiful. I show her the pictures and she laughs and smiles some more. It ends quickly but feels so good to hear it for the brief moment that it's there. I sit back down, still smiling to myself, feeling a lot lighter.

"She's seventeen," says Urbain from my left, pulling my smile back down. He's watching the ground as well. Urbain has been doing this work since the war began in 1996, but I can see that the stories still hurt him.

I shake my head and start writing in my notebook again. Maman Marie, Marcela, and the administrator resume their trio of talk.

She was raped last Thursday. So it's been four days. Today is the fourth day.

Another woman walks into the hospital room. She has the same distant look as Marcela. *You are worth so much*, I think to myself again. Timidly, she sits down on the bench next to me. Maman Marie shifts her focus and starts softly speaking with this woman. The woman looks a bit older than Marcela, and I find out she is twenty-eight years old. Her name is Devote, she is six months pregnant, and she was also raped four days ago.

She was on her way to get water when she was caught on the side of the road. They spoke Lingala and Swahili—governmental soldiers. She can't take medication for anything, not even for HIV prevention, because of the pregnancy.

The administrator lists off the facts as she says them. The word *they* cuts through the air like a high-pitched bell. I'm looking down at her hands fidgeting in her lap. I notice them start to quiver. When I look up, I see the tears in her eyes, but she's not letting them out.

I'm aching to tell her, *This doesn't change your worth in this world.*

I don't know how to say those words to her. I don't.

Devote is Marcela's older sister, I hear the administrator say. *Marcela is the youngest in the family.*

I can't think. I'm drowning in the desire to give these girls the things I have and would have access to if our roles were reversed: security, resources, help, and privilege.

They ask where they should go because even during the day the military are there.

Maman Marie explains that she will find a place for them to stay. Urbain brings in the last bags of food and blankets. Since our food supply is diminished in trying to help more people, I give them each four dollars, knowing that giving them any more than that would put them both in even more danger.

Their faces light up and the day, suddenly, is worthwhile.

Indira Allegra

SURVIVAL SEASON

Dear One,

The anniversary of your survival is on my calendar
a Veteran's Day for the war waged on women.

The anniversary of your survival is written right here
where journal pages tremble
against the anxiety of sleeping.

The anniversary of your survival is blue ink
drawing topographies of pleasure
blurred by fresh grief
gathered by arms of unsuspecting lovers.

The anniversary of your survival
every year, on this line, a horizon
where truth emerges from repetition
looping back to start the letter
your survival is written.

Choose Your Own
Adventure

Leah Lakshmi Piepzna-Samarasinha

SURVIVING ABUSE AS A CHOOSE YOUR OWN ADVENTURE NOVEL

Excerpts from Dirty River *by Leah Lakshmi Piepzna-Samarasinha*

This book is not *The Courage to Heal* and it's not *Push*. It's not *When You're Ready* or *No: A Woman's Word* or any of the other pastel incest books of the lesbian feminist '70s and '80s. It's not an incest horror story-book, and it's not palatable either. I don't get normal. I get something else.

There's uplift, but it ain't a straight shot. I'm not overcoming my terrible pain, my terrible horrible tragic lost innocent childhood. I'm not Sybil: The Woman With Three Personalities. My therapist is not a major character in it, and the therapy session, court dates, and talking with nice policemen, ditto.

This book is something else. It's the normality of it all. It's how running like fucking hell at twenty-one and living in a wall-to-wall shit-grey apartment at Dupont and Dufferin with a weedy leaning tree out back and a bunch of dandelions to eat for greens when you're broke, a shit-yellow fluorescent light, a bathtub, and a half-busted door that doesn't go up all the way but still locks, can feel like paradise. Can be fucking paradise.

The thing I always wanted to say is that surviving abuse sucks.

But it's also a Choose Your Own Adventure story.

It's also a true girl/boy adventure story. A heroic one.

The hero sets off on a journey of lockdown; screaming at Christmas/Eid/Pesach; fucked up yelling; a bus ticket; changing your phone number; writing that mammoth e-mail/letter and mailing it to your parents; poverty; buying towels; a Stable Girlfriend; everything falling apart again. Different generations of safe homes.

It's heroic. Not heartwarming.

It's probably the most classic hero story there is.

Throw in a little illegal immigration, sex work, brown-on-brown domestic violence and the struggle for social justice, plus a *Portrait of the Artist as a Young Queer Brown Femme*, and you've got something.

Some girls go to grad school. Some girls, in 1993, would go and type at $7.25-an-hour secretarial jobs. Me, I stuck my thumb out. I was going to move to Canada, work twenty hours a week at the prison-justice newspaper for free, do sex work, walk all over the city because I couldn't afford tokens, split a one-room apartment with my lover, make the revolution, have super abuse memories, see a barter feminist radical therapist, live on black beans and rice, try to learn to dance, go home.

Sometimes surviving abuse isn't terrible. Sometimes, when you leave your whole life behind, it feels like a Choose Your Own Adventure novel. Blissfully free, you stepping away from everything you've known. The bliss of your very first door that shuts all the way. Wind between your legs. Stopping everything that happened for seven generations.

Free. Free. Free.

Survivor Psychic Powers, Part One.

When I was a kid I could always tell who the survivor girls were. It was a special talent. Some kids played tennis or were really good at video games. I could look at the kids in the hall between classes and could tell who was being molested. Not that I could do anything about it, but I was never surprised.

Those girls—we fucked a lot behind the play structure or ate pencil shavings. Or were crazy, or were good, or set shit on fire, or were always so ironed down that you just couldn't stand looking at them because you knew that someday, that girlbomb would just blow. The girls who floated out of their skin, just begging someone to fucking notice. I didn't know why I could see. It hadn't happened to me, right? Just "emotional abuse," which is such a pussy concept.

In my family, my mother says, the women are psychic, just a little and just where it really counts. She was driving with my father and me one day when I was a baby, and they were at a stop sign about to roll, when she grabbed his arm for no reason and screamed, "*Roger!*" He was pissed, but right then out of nowhere a sky-blue Cadillac barreled through the light and would have smashed our car to bits. Another time she woke from a sound sleep, went downstairs without thinking about it, and saw that the pilot light had gone out and the kitchen was filling up with gas. I forget the third time. She says she thinks it's the ghost of her brother Johnny—her favorite brother, the sweet one, who made it home from Korea and got hit by a drunk driver a week later—looking out for her.

Her visions save her. Save us. Me, I can see who's been abused and I can see who's getting hit. I can tell who's puking in the girls' bathroom. I can see all this shit but I can't do shit about it except wait. I know that whole "this school is a jail" thing that was in *Pump Up the Volume* is a cliché of teenage rebellion but it really feels that way. I feel like I'm studying to gain skills about how to survive in the outside world. Getting ready and doing well on my APs so I can get early release.

But maybe incest was everywhere. In the tap water, in the air, in the mall. Every goddamn where. Every girl you knew. Maybe some of the boys, too. What would that mean if incest were everywhere? If every girl you knew told you shit in the basement of her house, whispering while you were watching *Children of the Corn* and eating Fritos, or told you by the way she turned her body in the locker room? But if you were her friend, you wouldn't tell anybody. Not nobody, not the school counselor or your mom. Saying it was worse. All you could do was hold the secret close.

The Amethyst Room

As soon as I'd seen the house, I thought, *yes*, and then, *everything will be okay here*. It was just a fucked up house on Dupont, smack in the middle of nowhere, right behind the railroad tracks and sandwiched in between a cement company and an auto-repair place. The CN high-power line was right behind the tracks, which gave it a kind of glow, and there was a tiny little 'ho stroll past the auto-repair, by some abandoned Portuguese social club. There wasn't much foot traffic on the streets, there was a bus stop right in front of my house, and the rush of cars sounded like the ocean. But it was a house, it had a back yard and a fence wild with grapes growing on it that I could hang a clothesline from, and it was perfect. A house in a narrow strip of six semi-detached houses that were all kind of leaning and fucked up in the middle of a mini zone of industrial waste. The door inside to my apartment didn't go up all the way and there was crappy carpet and a plastic brown and yellow kitchen, but there were two rooms with doors that shut, windows that looked out onto trees and railroad, and a big white bathroom with a big white bathtub and built-in shelves and moldings. Even before the shit went down, I knew it was my space. My house.

When I moved in after the week was up—when Jim passed the key to me with a grunt and I took the bus home—I walked up to it with my pink quilt, looking all around. I put my key in the lock, then in the other lock. I went up the stairs warily. I walked through all the rooms, looking up and around. I let out a deep breath. I was alone, and the door was locked, and only I had the key.

My bedroom was a room like an altar in the middle of the broken-down house. Amethyst like the colors of the womb I would've grown inside if I'd had a colored mother. That was how I thought of it. A lumpy plum double-futon picked off the street with the duvet I hauled with me on the floor. Big wardrobe that was left there before I moved in, that made me feel rich, groaning open. No furniture. Milk crates. Things that were taken from junk.

This was where I dreamed for hours. The train hooting by on the Canadian Pacific rail tracks out back, running parallel to Dupont. The bathroom window opened into the wild backyard jungle. Burdock plants, wild grape, dandelion, narrow bands of dirt that grow peas, lettuce, and greens. Motherwort, to-matillos, tomatoes, a wild shaggy weed tree. All the cats that twined, twenty or more by the tracks. The hooting of the train.

I dreamed for hours. It felt unreal and sick, how it took me four hours to get off the futon to go to the bathroom. I took hot baths with sea salt to pull everything toxic out of my body.

This was my first home. The first place I could shut the door and when I did, everything would exhale.

I tried to find this place for years in New York. Even pre-*Sex in the City* ultra gentrification I could never afford anything. Three hundred dollars a month was my cap. They wouldn't rent to me as a student on financial aid with a Barnes and Noble job and parents who were helping out. But I pictured a railroad flat, three little rooms glowing yellow, and a door that shut.

This place was like a womb where I regrew myself. A starfish. Someone in neonatal.

I dreamed for hours again. Slept for hours, and sleep was like a rose coverlet I pulled over my head.

The night before I put the twenty-two-page ma-nila envelope in the mail, I had this dream: I was floating in the sky. Way up in the inky black. I could feel all the ancestors around me, hovering. I asked them, "Is what I think about my parents, about everything, true?" I didn't hear, but felt, the word *yes* slamming into my body. Echoing from everywhere around me. And then I was falling, so many millions of miles, an hour back down. I woke with a thump as I fell back down on the bed.

There stabbing pains in my cunt. There are times when I feel myself at three walking next to me. That girl, her short legs, growing-out soft bowl cut, soft

huge hazel eyes, both all the way present and disas
sociated. I walk the alleyways. I hold her hand.

Healing Mix Tape

Bikini Kill: "Demirep"
African Head Charge: "Heading to Glory"
Fun-da-mental: "Mother Africa Feeding Sister India"
    and "Wrath of the Black Man"
John Trudell: anything from *Blue Indians* or *Johnny
    Damas & Me*
Asian Dub Foundation: "Naxalite"
Joy Harjo: "For Anna Mae Pictou Aquash"
Buffy Sainte Marie: "I'm Going Home"
Method Man and Mary J. Blige: "All I Need"
Tribe Called Quest: "Stressed Out"
Meshell Ndgeocello: "Ecclesiastes: Free My Heart"

Made It Home: 2012

I am thirty-six and have arrived here. Life has tak-
en me to a big, crooked house on Stuart Street in
Southwest Berkeley, to the crip, queer, femme, majority of-color house of my dreams. It is my good dream.
It is part of how I healed. A Taurus survivor girl, I
dreamed this big house full of color, burnt orange
and magenta walls, bookshelves spilling over, notices
tacked to the fridge, and bulletin board of parties,
benefits, childhood photos, and current photos of
housemates hugging on each other. My pictures tend
to look like this. In my Facebook photos, I am, nine
times out of ten, hugging on some friend, lover, or
fam. My photos shout over and over again, *I made it,
I am not alone, I am loved, loved, loved.*

My house is full of big messy garden with curvy-sided beds, a magnolia tree, a camellia bush, and plum and fig and walnut trees. Big sacks of food on the shelves lining the kitchens, multiple washer-dryers, all our various weird cars out front. On good days, it is the house of my dreams: the Delney-style compound where housemates run in and out, cooking greens, checking in about lovers and weeks and mental- and physical health, throwing money for food in the house jar, cooking from the thirty-six pack of free-range eggs on the bottom of the kitchen table I bought.

I am thirty-six and I have landed in and co-created this safe, femme, of-color survivor home. And this is why, this is where, I can write my father for Christmas and be happy when he writes me back the same week, sending me a card in a shiny gold envelope. Because I am his daughter, and we both have excellent taste and love shiny and gold. Because we are both gay. That man who taught me how to find a Brooks Brothers suit on quadruple markdown in a TJ Maxx. This is where I can fall in love with someone who can meet me, who can touch me, who is not afraid to claim me as their lover in public. This is why I am prettier than I was two years ago, at thirty-six with white hair and the beginning of browngirl whatthefuck lines between my eyebrows. I am lovely. I made my way home. I made this home.

Denise Santomauro

LETTER 20: A JEANS-WEARING DREAMER

Dear You,

I can't even begin to express how happy I am to be writing this. To get the chance to actually be a part of this movement for hope? Well, hot damn! Sign me up.

My work brings me in direct contact with child survivors, and the thing I see over and over again is the resilience of the human spirit. I have watched children transform in front of my eyes, from being overwhelmed with the weight of their reality one minute, to their eyes lighting up when the person they love more than themselves walks into the room. Watching them play and laugh after such a horrific ordeal is a constant reminder that nothing is permanent. Change is inevitable. For some, it happens in mere minutes. For others, it takes days or weeks. Sometimes even years pass before we notice it. But change will come.

Recently I was talking with my mother about the differences between our childhood experiences, and this idea of change became quite clear through one seemingly insignificant detail from her teen years:

"So, I read something odd the other day," I casually said to her. "I had no idea that women's sports were so regulated when you were in high school."

"Oh, yeah," she exclaimed. "There was only cheerleading. No other sports. Also, we weren't allowed to wear pants."

"What!" I was dumbfounded at the idea of my new hip-hugging, dark-wash blues being tucked away in a drawer and my never getting the chance to flaunt my curves.

"Uh huh. It was a big scandal at my school when they finally allowed girls to wear slacks. It wasn't until I was a senior. My father still wouldn't let me though," she laughed.

Small detail, yes, but oh, how the times have changed. So it makes me ask, if it was scandalous for girls in the 1960s to wear pants to school, what else will we look back on and shake our heads at? What else can't we see in the future? And at that, what else can we dream up?

For me, I dream of a world fighting to end sexual assault and abuse, one where survivors are championed for their courage. I dream of recovery, for all survivors, and can envision a collective agreement to support that long, hard, misunderstood battle with an embracing and loving patience. And in my wildest, most indulgent dreams, we only hear about sexual assault and abuse in history books.

And why not? Why can't that world be a reality? Resiliency should be the motto for the human race. We have the ability to survive all manner of circumstances that, in theory, should obliterate us. Nature constantly comes up with new diseases and hazards to stand in our way. And we basically give it all the finger.

We are survivors. That's our greatest ability. Don't forget it.

Love,
A jeans-wearing dreamer

Maroula Blades

I ACHE

I've been aching since the day I was born,
Dropped bloody by a nurse in the hospital.
Ma spine's crooked; I just missed being dense.
Ma brother's good to me, talks to me he does.

I've been aching since the day I was born,
I asked ma uncle if I was pretty,
He said, "Let me feel you where you grow,
Lawd, you're pretty all right like a plump peach."

I've been aching since the day I was born,
Mama shoved me in the attic, visitors came,
I was scared. I was cold. I hate ebony spiders.
I waved coldly to people's backs through cracks.

I've been aching since the day I was born.
I asked a well-dressed priest, "Why is it so?"
He said, "God works in mysterious ways,
His ways are not our ways."

I've been aching since the day I was born,
Aches as I scrub Mr. Dixon's floor for coins,
Aches as I wring Mrs. Bell's sheets for nothing,
Battle aches as Joe touches me, his "beast gal."
Aches, one dull, heavy ache after another,

Scaly hands, bent bones, nothing but gruel.
I'm gonna hang this ill-fitting skin out to dry,
Go around bloody doing Carrie take-offs.
I'm gonna jump into the skin of a zebra,
Lovely like a Zulu shield, spear red soil with ma breath,
Back strong against the brawny wind,
Eat plenty; stamp mangrove with ma hooves, free.

Melissa Gordon

LETTER 21: SURVICTIM

Dear Sister,

"Survictim." That's what I was told I had become after my rape. Which is funny because I wasn't aware that I was required to label myself as anything new. Everywhere I had turned for comfort, I had someone telling me that my life, at eighteen years old, would now be defined as pre- and post-rape. I may as well have hung a sign around my neck. There was no dream large enough to overshadow this, no light bright enough to chase away its darkness. I was a statistic.

"Survictim." What a wicked, amorphous word. What a minimizing, condescending, made up, bullshit word. I couldn't hang my fear on it and couldn't give it my shame, my anger, my newfound paranoia, my isolation. All it meant was that I wasn't me anymore, and that was the worst part. I was suddenly drowning in a new identity, an identity that had been forced on me, and I didn't know how I was supposed to live with that.

All that I'd believed about myself before my rape simply didn't exist anymore. I had been a proud virgin, but I wasn't that anymore. I had been proud of being a good judge of character, but it turned out that someone who I thought I could trust raped me. I could no longer lay claim to anything about myself. And yet, I claim my rape as my own. I refer to the incident as "my rape." Never "the rape." I own it. I had heard about survivors who never healed, who were perceived as damaged goods to be looked at, pitied, and discarded. I was to be someone else's cautionary tale. It was my body, my virginity, my burden.

Not once did anyone tell me that I might be all right after I stopped bleeding, after the bruises healed. No one told me that there might be a day when I wouldn't think about it anymore. So, what I want to tell you is that liberation is possible after a rape. I won't tell you that everything will be neat and tidy. Your journey will be distinctly yours. Yes, you are changed, but how you change is entirely up to you. Isn't that a wonder?

Sister, don't be afraid of what happens next. Don't pretend to be happy and don't be silent if that's not who you are. Embrace every feeling, grieve if you need to, rejoice when you want. You aren't wrong for feeling anything that you feel. This experience was wholly yours, and whatever you take from it is entirely in your possession. You were someone special before this happened and that light has not been extinguished.

For me, twelve years after my rape, I have found a lot of things that I thought I had lost. I'm a teacher, and I don't know that I would have found that calling had I not gone through the journey I did after my rape. I found the strength to stand in front of a room full of teenagers and let them see who I really am. I realized how worthy I am of living a life that suits my needs.

I found God again. I found that my laugh was not stuck in my throat and happiness was not a lost cause. I even found that day when my mom actually acknowledged what happened to me instead of calling it a "youthful indiscretion."

The day will come when you realize that this does not define your life. You may sigh, you may smile, and you may even cry. But you'll have lived through it and have made it through to the other side. You will know that you are loved and beloved. And maybe then you'll write a letter, too.

I wish you all the peace and all the love you need to carry on through this life.

Melissa

adrienne maree brown

AWAKENING

i have spent over half of my life responding to sexual trauma, both my own and others'. i am now deep into my healing journey, into loving myself. i have slowly come to know myself as a beautiful, powerful creative—a writer, as well as a facilitator, a healer, and a doula.

i made it this far and i want to tell you how. transparency about my healing process helps me to be more whole.

someone recently taught me that everything we do to survive is smart. shifting from seeing so many of my actions not as failing but as intelligence has been magnificent and hard. here's how i was smart, how i survived long enough to fall in love with myself:

first, i gained weight. looking back, i think i didn't want anyone looking at me. at the time i wasn't aware of it, but i just suddenly felt a dependency and longing for the comfort of chocolate, pizza, bread. when i would try to lose weight, as soon as my body started changing, as soon as people started paying attention, i would return to eating.

i worked too much—i left no time to have a relationship or intimacy. before i was an adult, i'd become an expert at surviving the present, being able to move into contact with people without feeling, without letting them close to me.

i went to see a therapist in college because i was depressed. i'd blocked my trauma thoroughly, so i felt ridiculous, because i didn't know why i was so sad all the time. i couldn't explain it, couldn't trace it. the sessions would entail me sitting there unable to get to the root of my feelings, feeling like i was disappointing to and misunderstood by the educated, successful, skinny/healthy nice white woman who really wanted to make sure i wasn't going to be another suicide statistic for the school. i became an expert at faking a smile for a few sessions, and then i stopped going. it was easier to drink.

most people don't make it to therapy the first time, so it's a minor miracle that i agreed to go the second time, about five years later.

i'd been engaging in all manner of self-harm in the spirit of doing nice indulgent things for myself…i ate too much, drank too much, smoked too much. i cast a haze over myself.

i'd learned to measure and respond to the desire of other people for my touch and my body, without feeling any desire in me. i became a pleasure giver. my mind knew that i was supposed to be having sex at this age, so i leaned into that without much awakening in my body in response to flirtations and lovers.

i even cut myself to see if i was real.

and when i felt nothing, i fell down into the darkness of that feeling, which was deep and all-encompassing.

the second therapist had been mentioned in conversation with a black woman i trusted. she said she had gone and was actually going to stop because she wasn't yet ready to do the work this therapist was asking her to do.

a few months later, i found myself at the edge of a metaphorical plank with my family and friends all looking out at me with that look in their eyes, that edge to their voices, the unique combination of fear and insecurity that loved ones get when they are trying to save someone's life and have no idea how. and i remembered this woman's name.

praise whoever made that gentle black woman therapist, whose office smelled of lavender and was always a shade too cool.

i went in with a bit more trust than the first time— this was no school-assigned therapist, this was someone who had been vouched for by someone i trusted. still, for the first few visits, i did what i learned my first time around in therapy. i insisted i wasn't suicidal even though i was secretly seeing exit plans everywhere and had already tried; i said i wasn't interested in medications so she wouldn't think i was scamming; i generally said things i thought sounded healthy.

and i watched her as she didn't buy it. she would purse her lips, lift her eyebrows, sometimes even make scoffing sounds.

she didn't sit there just listening, and she didn't let me slip out the door without letting me know two things: one, that i stank of bullshit, and two, that she was excited to see me in a couple of days.

after we got through that, the work began.

she remembered everything i told her and would actually help draw connections and patterns out of my stories, things i wasn't seeing in terms of my agency and power.

she said things to me like "we will get you through this," and "you are such a good person."

she wasn't afraid to reference her own experiences discreetly—and she had relevant experiences. this mattered to me—i hate sharing my pain with people who give me nothing back—it makes me feel like entertainment, except on my own dime. i have met people who seem to get something healing or safe from being the center of attention for their suffering, but that has never made me feel comfortable.

i like to have my shit together and define "together" with all the virgo precision i can muster.

the combination of her blackness, her calm, her sense of having emotional reference points—of having survived—her ability to laugh and meet my fears, all of this slowly got me to open as much as i was able to at that point in my life.

i saw her over the next three years, stopping when i felt i didn't need therapy—not because i was healed but because i was able to see myself clearly without the container of therapy. and then i came back when i would lose my sense of self.

she was consistent with me.

i think a lot of who i *was* shocked her, but she smiled through it and stayed present and i am grateful to her forever.

she asked me questions i didn't want to answer—like whether i was using sex as a way to avoid intimacy. she let the question sit there while i danced all around it. later when i stilled enough to answer, she helped me enter my first healing period of celibacy.

this came after a period of random sexual encounters that went horribly awry, including a confrontation with a surprise baby mama, another with a surprise fiancé, a messy night with someone who became a comrade, and a violent encounter with someone i thought i loved.

i realized i was having sex to feel better and sexier, to feel whole, and it was actually not working that way at all—it was making me feel lonely and sloppy.

i had also developed a skill for acting and pretending in bed that didn't serve me. i evaluated the greatness of a sexual encounter by how blown away my sexual partner was. my pleasure wasn't centered in my physical experience.

so, celibacy.

i had heard of it.

the first thing i noticed in my first celibacy was that i had been sexualizing almost every experience; with friends, with friends' partners, with coworkers, with strangers on the train...i had been building a sort of prison of sex, and there was no space outside of it.

i wanted so desperately to be sexually normal that i had turned it into an obsession.

once i decided not to have it for a while, a world of other kinds of interactions opened up. it was powerful to realize that there could be passion in politics and in friendship that wasn't a veiled foreplay.

i did nice things for myself during that time—it was my first time having a digital camera and i conducted my first self-portraiture project. i started to learn my face and body and judge them for myself, not just on a scale of whether someone else wanted me.

when i was ready to have sex again, i found a lover that i could really feel my desire for, who was sweet, kind, and cared if i was enjoying it. then, the next lover i took ended up being one of the great loves of my life. i deeply believe that period of celibacy gave me the space to realize i was lovable, a major step on my healing journey.

my therapist also helped me identify healthier coping mechanisms—practices to get me through my lost days. she listened to me, constantly giving me a sense that she believed i had a future where i wouldn't be suffering. the idea—that healing would take time and come later, and that I deserved to make it to later—was liberating.

it felt spacious.

my life has been riddled with things i didn't want to see, couldn't imagine, or couldn't remember. the main coping mechanism that she helped me identify was writing, constantly—emotional portraits in the form of poems, songs, political rants, love notes. writing is a major part of how i heal.

i also sang a lot, mostly in private. i discovered science fiction and lost myself in alternate universes and the future.

i was particularly drawn to fluid representations of gender and sexuality—i think reading octavia butler reawakened my desire. i loved the idea that attraction and intimacy could be safe, beautiful, liberating, energetic—that everyone involved could be powerful.

i was still overeating and overworking, but i started to say yes to healing things, which included going to healing places that i was invited to; going to purpose-oriented leadership development programs; environmentalism; getting massages, reiki, and craniosacral therapy—and love.

love, being loved, was so healing.

it also illuminated that i still had work to do in and with my body.

around the time i realized this, i began to learn

about somatics, the study of the whole self—mind, body, and spirit—paying particular attention to what the body knows and holds, letting the body be a space for healing trauma.

body, a space for healing.

i couldn't remember having a positive association with my body.

learning to tune into and love my body has reshaped how i remember my life, how i remember my pain. i can tell if i am withdrawing and afraid, or if I am centered, self-loving, calm, and grounded. it is radical and it is a sign of healing that i can feel these things again, in my body.

I recently had another period of celibacy in which I built off the lessons of the first one. I created a delicious world of desire and pleasure, letting the attention of others flow into my growing desire for myself instead of displacing it. now I think of myself as the greatest lover of my life. I make decisions from a place of what is right for me when I am loving myself.

and of course, there are things that i have only been able to remember through my body. times when only standing there, bent over the bed and weeping, letting the whole pain of my past sweep through me, and letting my body release it, could i feel whole again.

somatics and transformative writing and people supporting me and crying and purpose and love and therapy. while i was in it i thought of it as a healing journey. now i think that love is what was distorted for me, love is what was taken from me, the sense that i was valuable and lovable.

so i think of all of this as my self-love journey.

i am still on that journey, and i will keep calling my story out as i grow and learn.

and i am so in love with myself.

"all that you touch you change. all that you change, changes you. the only everlasting truth is change—god is change."
—octavia butler—

Isabella Gitunu-Woolf

OUR ANCESTORS WERE WATCHING

Our ancestors were watching
while you were raping their daughters
leaving them with tears
of acid rain
weeping of the pain
we should have never tasted
trying to get us to suckle
their nipples of nourishment
but only sour on our tongues
only blood flows
drowning us as they
watch in disbelief as they throw us a life raft
of "it wasn't your fault"
that we just let float by
because we can't recognize even
a thread of familiar
you left us with nothing
but wounds that won't heal
and voices that were silenced
be silent
or I will kill you
and when that didn't work
because he understood
the death within me
be silent

or I will kill your mother
Ancestors! Mother Kali! Mamata! My kin!
where are you, my Mothers?
I can't see you in my dark
give me strength!
and the next time he blocked my way
with groping hands
and poison on his breath
I was not silent
no! I will kill you!
the warrior spirit crept in
but I could not look her in the eye
she spiraled herself in and through my ribs
entangling herself within my womb
and hid there
I turned my back then
on my Mothers
pretending they didn't exist
pretended my warrior
was not hiding inside
how am I to be loved now?
how am I loved without being fucked?
and so on my search
for love and wholeness
I filled my emptiness
with fucks and licks and sucks
hoping, praying I would be filled
yet I remained
hollow.
empty.
unloved.
until the one day
I realized
that I could love

myself.
I held that love in my
heart and womb
my Ancestors rejoiced
I held that love
in my mouth, in my breasts, in my pussy
my Ancestors rejoiced
I took the love I felt for me and
reclaimed my body, my spirit, my voice
I take back my heart and womb
my Mothers dance
I heal my mouth, my breasts, my cunt
bringing the Goddess back to her rightful place
my Mothers dance
my Mothers sing
my Mothers tell me that now I am free
I am free!
my body now restored as a temple
where a Goddess resides
the curve of my breast
is gilded in the finest gold
the sway of my ass
is draped in silks
my belly is painted in crimson red
and my toes are in purple
the temple of my body
my body as my temple
sex as my magic
magic as my sex
I see myself in the reflection in my lover's eyes
knowing then as my body
cums to the rhythm inside
I know another layer of freedom
and my Mothers dance

and they sing to the song of
letting go and surrendering
not to my lover
but to myself
my body is a temple
and you worship at the alter of my feet
opening me in ways I didn't know existed
I take my lover's nipple in my mouth
and drink the sweet milk of my Ancestors
I turn your acid rain into a
flowing river between my legs
of wet water and earth
that you taste on your tongue
like communion
of our Mothers' bodies and of our Mothers' blood
I stand now in my power
and I dance to the beat of the drum inside
that I never lost but found again
and I sing
I sing the song
I am not a victim
I am not a survivor
I am a phoenix rising above my own ashes
I am a warrior
I am a warrior of the Mother line
reclaiming the cunts of her daughters
and my Mothers dance
and my Mothers sing
along with me.

Sofia Rose Smith & Lisa Factora-Borchers

THE PLACE OF FORGIVENESS: A CONVERSATION

It was never going to be easy, this topic of forgiveness. There's no formula, strategy, or even a universal language to speak about it. To engage the question of forgiveness alone on a page is like knitting a scarf with only one needle. There are some things that take two to weave together.

After thousands of words had been written, endless rounds of edits and try-agains, Sofia texted Lisa,

It's way easier to talk about forgiveness than to write about it solitarily. Forgiveness is a possibility that happens in conversation…

The simplicity of the point cut through the layers of questioning and doubts that Lisa had about format. Forgiveness, with its winding and sinewy nature, is a possibility that arises in a clearing, or a field. That clearing/place becomes possible in conversation with another person. We guide one another. When alone, the darkness may be overwhelming, but with another person, a seedling breaks open.

Sofia and Lisa's conversation on forgiveness began on a warm, sunny September afternoon in Los

Angeles, California, sitting in Sofia's garden, under a crying ficus tree. It continued across different time zones, over e-mails, writing prompts, FaceTime, phone calls, and text messages. This was our process to ask a question that neither of us could precisely answer: what is forgiveness after sexual violence, or what is the place of forgiveness for survivors?

To write and, more importantly, to read this, it will be helpful to review these three affirmations. The following supported us in creating this piece as an offering.

- Accept this spiritual body of writing as you accept your own life: with limitations, fragmentation, imperfection, and possibility. We respond with our life experiences and perspectives, which may or may not address your needs or feel true to you.

- Consider the multi-dimensional and self-defined nature of forgiveness. It can only come from you, when the need to grow outweighs the pain of possibility.

- Remember that who, what, whether, where, and how you forgive is entirely in your possession.

From here, this dialogue begins. Thank you for entering into it with us.

Lisa: *So we venture into something that has no beginning and no end, right? Forgiveness. We think we know what it is, but in our experiences, it has its own life. It's* *been defined as "forgive and forget," "let go," "it's okay." But those terms don't work for everyone. Kind of like justice. There are so many ways to view it. Maybe we start there. Before asking about forgiveness, we interrogate justice.*

Sofia: Justice. Yes. What is justice? I believe in the possibility of transformative justice.[2] Ten years ago, when I survived rape, I didn't report my assault. My older sister asked if I wanted to go to the hospital that night, but I said no, and scoffed, and drove home toward the new pain, the different world that would open to me. At times I regret not having gone. I will not lie and tell you that I don't. And yet, as life opened up to me after my survival, and as I began to grow and integrate so many lessons from my survival, and so many new lenses through which I saw the world, I realized that the spirit of Sofia has never believed in the criminal (in)justice system as it is set up in the US.

A deeper part of me always knew that the criminal

---

2   There are many definitions of transformative justice. Please journey through these meanings and possibilities. Here are some websites that provide a starting place: http://www.phillystandsup.com/tj.html and http://www.generationfive.org/tj.php. There's also a bit of a difference between transformative and restorative justice, some of which can be read about here: http://thesocietypages.org/sociologylens/2013/03/05/restorative-justice-and-transformative-justice-definitions-and-debates/. Here is an organization based in Oakland that engages in restorative justice work with youth: http://www.nccdglobal.org/blog/meet-our-staff-sujatha-baliga-leads-nccd-s-new-restorative-justice-project.

justice system (top-down or vertical, as opposed to horizontal or communal) trying my rapist would not solve the problem of my rape in the world. I don't know that it would have granted me peace. I don't know that it would have helped me achieve this question of forgiveness that arises in my mind on occasion. I doubt that my perpetrator would have been held accountable in a way that transformed him, or me, or the world. So then I wonder what some alternative models of justice could have looked like. And I know there are many beautiful humans engaged in envisioning this as we speak, like generationFIVE, though I didn't know that at the time of my rape.

L: *Accountability. I think its absence creates the most grief.*

S: Yes, for survivors I think that can be true. There is a complex grief that we experience as survivors. For me, my grief had to do with loss (loss of self, loss of the world as a place that did no harm). For whatever our grief is, it's critical that we find ways to honor and experience our grief, whether through our tears, or prayer, or activism, or art, or community. I metabolized my grief through dance, yoga, writing, studying, tears, therapy, meditation, and conversation, and yet it was somehow a very solitary experience. I remember that the first time I lost a loved one, my Lakota teacher suggested we have a sweat ceremony called a Wiping of the Tears. During those many hours of ceremony, I cried and cried, sweat and sweat, sang and sang. I had tied a hundred prayers with tobacco and burned them. I had sat by the river and let it calm me. I drank from a bowl of my tears, and my community drank my tears from that same bowl, and we grieved together, and they were with me in loss, and they bore witness to my brokenness. Until then, I had no models for grieving, for letting go, or for giving away. And I remember thinking that for survivors, this kind of communal grieving and acknowledgement of our losses would have been (and are) so healing. And I say this solemnly, not wishing to re-appropriate or commodify First Nations' practices, but to acknowledge how blessed I was to experience what grief in community looks, tastes, sounds, and feels like.

L: *And grief is cyclical. Grief isn't one torrent, ever-present cloud of pressure. It's more like a traveling rainstorm. It comes and goes, seemingly never-ending, but it ends for a time. Departs. Then comes a brilliant blue-sky day. Then a windy day arrives. The rain comes back and after a while, you begin to learn to read the signs of its coming and better anticipate the storm. Nonetheless, it can still sometimes feel like the first time you've seen a droplet and are terrified because you fear drowning in the flood since you never learned how to swim.*

S: I love that, yes, so true. As survivors, we are also surviving our grief. We survive the years of questions that being a survivor might create—questions that often go unanswered. And sometimes I wonder if our perpetrators don't somehow, in some way, experience a trajectory of subtle grief as well, as spiritual beings who caused harm to other spiritual beings.

We've survived so much, and I wonder if it's possible to move beyond survival into a new space of identification where we are neither survivor nor victim; where we aren't necessarily defined in relation to our perpetrator, but instead exist on a continuum with them as part of our humanness; where those distinctions above don't exist; where we are with them, our perpetrators; where we are "both/and" as opposed to "either/or"; where dichotomy and binary aren't relevant; where we are of them, and they are of us.

L: *I love that: "beyond survival." That was the name of an advocacy center I worked at for survivors. I thought about it for years, asking, "What does it mean to move beyond survival?" I never got my answer. Maybe it's an undocumented arena that needs to be named.*

I like but feel uncertain about the oneness you just referenced. That's intense because there's a very real part of our physical and mental trauma that cannot comprehend oneness because sometimes survival is dependent on the separation of danger and safety, a separation from the attempted spiritual murder. Sometimes that separation is integral to survival.

S: Yes. I want to be careful around that concept. Survivors need to unapologetically do what they need to do in order to survive, and in the initial stages of healing, I don't think forgiveness is the right question to be pondering. It's just not a consideration. It's not healthy if they're not ready.

L: *Right. So we're talking about the possibility of forgiveness when a survivor feels psychologically, emotionally, and physically safe to explore the possibility of what violence means in a larger context.*

S: Yes, and this isn't going to fit everyone. This is just another pathless way to heal, to process violence in a larger context. And when that time comes, if it comes, one way to break open the idea of forgiveness is by pondering what it even is. What are some other words for forgiveness? For me, "I am another you. *In lak'ech*," made sense.

L: *I am another you.*

S: The moment our perpetrators assaulted us, even before that, they became a part of us. I know that healing takes place when the survivor reclaims their body from their perpetrator's grasp, but I also wonder if it's helpful for me to think of myself as victim/survivor and to think of my perpetrator as the evil criminal. I can think of him as criminal, because he did assault me through a criminal act that really, truly fragmented me mentally, physically, and spiritually. It was terrible, it tore me apart, I bled. My blood was on him. There was terror in his eyes. He carries this with him; his spirit carries this with him. I want him to heal and I also want him to feel pain, and this is human of me.

And think of it this way: Our bodies remember. On a cellular level they remember our trauma. Somehow, then, our perpetrators do remain with us on a cellular, psychical, spiritual level. And, until they heal from their wretchedness (I'm hesitant to even call it "their wretchedness" because I don't want to hyperbolize their criminality), can we ever fully heal ourselves? We probably can, but it's a question for me, nonetheless.

L: *I don't have other words for forgiveness, I just know that there is a space between or maybe beyond forgiveness; a place that is not quite fully imagined yet. So, instead of trying to name it, I try to think of the things that impede*

*our walk to get there, in the hope that we can name it once
we find it. I think about our cultural norms that try to tell
us how to heal and be satisfied with the hole it leaves us
with when judicial processes fail to heal us.*

*So much dogma defines justice by the concept of frac-
ture. We fracture the relationship between survivor and
perpetrator so we know who's who. We need separation to
have a sense of order. Our society uses fractures for order
and identity. "They"—the dangerous ones—are separate
from "us." Perpetrators of violence belong somewhere else,
not with us, because the alternative would be to consider
including them in the healing process and that is not a
popular notion to embrace. We're all broken—survivors,
allies, families, communities—and then we inflict further
fracture on the brokenness, hoping to find wholeness.*

S: Yes. You have to be ready to expand forgiveness
so it's not just about one person's healing, but about
envisioning a society where this doesn't happen. They,
the perpetrators, are part of that process. Their healing is integral. *If* they were healed, they would be the
ones writing the prevention books, facilitating workshops, abolishing systems of oppression, and teaching
love. Accountability. There are no maps for this, no
pathways, only pathlessness.

L: *That's incredible to think about. So much healing revolves around the image of a path, or there being a certain "way" to go about it. Instead of being intuitively
led, we search for "The Path." I wonder if the process of
forgiveness is less about finding a path and more about
revealing its pathlessness.*

*So in our need to heal, we first seek out justice, right?
We look for a way to right what was wrong, to recover a*

sense of what was lost. But is that even really possible? What is lost is lost. What if we didn't focus on hunting what can never be recovered and instead focused on building something new? Many survivors are left without systematic justice. And it leads me to question the mainstream notions of justice and reparation and whether they truly bring peace.

S: I agree that what is lost is lost. In the early stages of my survival, I wanted to somehow recover my innocence, and then, slowly, I realized that I had lost part of myself, and I began my grief from there. I mean, when we lose loved ones, we must confront that we cannot recover them in body. We can continue to speak with them, though; they are there, and that can be recovery, too.

I've read that in some First Nations traditions, a perpetrator of violence would be in a ceremonial process of accountability, which would honor the oneness of the whole community. They would not be removed or isolated from the community, not imprisoned or kept away. They would be engaged in healing, they would drink from the medicine of teachers, they would be asked to understand the suffering they caused in another being. Kind of like *in lak ech:* when one is harmed, we are all harmed. Of course, this kind of model still relies on survivors being safe enough to raise our voices, which is rare in a world that asks us to be silent. Our liberation and our peace rely heavily on our strength to resist our oppressions. I would argue, too, that the systems of power we live in depend on our perpetrators being and staying broken. It depends on folks being disempowered (including us), even if the legal system operates on the pretense of mending what's broken.

We all live within interlocking systems of oppression: the prison industrial complex, the criminal (in)justice system, the law, the non-profit industrial complex, all of which depend on systems of power and categorical, hierarchical structures. The law, for example, doesn't have any kind of intersectional analysis and instead simplifies humans to singular identity-based categories (for example, race-based hate crime or gender-based hate crime, as opposed to both simultaneously), erasing the subtleties of our experiences of oppression. I cannot honor my own complexity within any of these systems that ask me to exist only in the binaries. What kind of system is that? Not one that creates the possibility of healing justice.

L: *Totally. Forgiveness isn't binary. It's the antithesis of binary. In forgiveness, there is an exploration of possibility, possibility to move into fresh self-efficacy. That kind of possibility needs a lot of space to experiment. Forgiveness is sold under an illusion of linearity, like a one-stop decision, but it's just not that cut and dried at all. Our Western culture is obsessed with straight and clear processes—boxes of milestones we check off to prove we are "normal," "okay," "clear," "identifiable"—when, in fact, no one is okay because we're all healing in some form. We're all suffering in some way, and to truly liberate ourselves, to freely forgive ourselves, our perpetrators, the bystanders, the ones we thought should have protected us, we have to consider the limitations of binary relationship: survivor/perpetrator, good/evil, yes/no, free/enslaved. And if we see beyond binaries, we may consider a process that includes the perpetrator in the healing process.*

S: We learn that certain harm is valid. We live in a world that continues to enslave us by placing whole human beings in cages. Prison is commonplace; it is an assumed, hegemonic presence from a very young age. Some 2.3 million souls are incarcerated, half of whom are black.[3] The Hershey's chocolate we place on our tongues comes from cocoa plantations farmed by child slaves all along the Ivory Coast. These children sleep in cages at night. Is it any wonder, in this context of so much violence, that there would be the insidious existence of sexual violence, too? Is it any wonder we live in a rape culture?

That's what I mean by that we co-exist with harm. Alongside it. Inside it. This is the world of being human. And we must not turn away from it. It is why we must be engaged in multi-issue movements to end violence of all kinds: to abolish the prison, to abolish continued slavery, to dismantle racism and classism and ableism and transphobia/homophobia, to rise like dandelions against the systems that uproot us. We only grow back stronger.[4] We must be engaged with coalitions that work together to end the systems that oppress and enslave us and we must be the communal creation of new possibilities for freedom. We must be willing to dream big enough, to imagine what justice and liberation could be.

---

3 This information about the Ivory Coast and the figure of 2.3 million comes from Mark-Anthony Johnson—poet, healer, and activist.

4 For more information on #RiseOfTheDandelions, see the art and organizing work of Patrisse Culors-Brignac, founder and Executive Director of the Coalition to End Sheriff Violence in LA Jails (www.facebook.com/EndSheriffViolenceInLAJails).

So, no, maybe it's not about forgiveness. Maybe it's not.

But maybe it's about recognizing that none of us are free until all of us are free. None of us are free until there are no cages, there is no rape, and there is no violence. We are complicit with the roads that killed the earth. We are complicit with the harming of the animals that feed us. We may disagree with the principles of capitalism that create the matrix of oppression we live in, but we live in it. We act for change and transformation, sure, but all of us still do harm in some ways, some days, some hows. None of us are free from it, from harming or being harmed, from being oppressor and oppressed simultaneously.

And, none of us are free from the myth of separateness that first initiates this possibility of harm. I'm interested in harm reduction, sure. But I'm quite a bit more interested in the possibility that we can do no harm.

L: *I was raised on Filipino Catholicism, a religious backbone that taught us to turn the other cheek, to pray for them, and when asked how many times to forgive, we were to forgive seventy times seventy times seventy. There were many aspects that I took literally. There were elements of it that felt pious and truthfully disproportionate to the depth of human suffering. Is forgiveness an absolution you grant after a solo tour de grace? I don't think so. I think it can be much more than that. It needs to be more than just an absolution or time done in jail.*

S: Then what do you think this looks like? How do we create visions of healing outside of these systems?

L: *Well, it's clear from our talks and work that the question* *of forgiveness doesn't come without other questions. It asks for nuanced definitions of justice, healing, and, ultimately, love. Forgiveness isn't an absolution, but may be revisited states of balance. From time to time, we leave that state of balance to question and probe a bit more—which makes us uncomfortable, but we do it to regain a deeper balance.*

To build this healing outside systems of separateness, binary, linear thinking, and entrapment, I think the first step is to be open to the possibility that the current judicial system offers one way to potentially heal, but that it often fails us. We have to accept that violence, at its core, is the act of taking power from someone by asserting more power. And our very liberation stands on our ability to examine the grounds of that dynamic. At our deepest spiritual levels, are we able to examine our notions and abuses of power?

I think that we need to be fearless in the face of saying that perhaps there is no justice available to survivors in the way we have come to define it. There is no evening out of the playing field. There is no lost and found here. There is courage and open land space to rebuild, and if we are able to move beyond the binary, the perpetrator would be included in that rebuilding.

S: Right. And this is just a beginning. Barely tapping the well of the possibility of forgiveness, in the context of togetherness or oneness.

What if our perpetrator is us? And not in a woo-woo, New Age hippie way, but in an ancestral way. In a way that remembers a time when we were one and breathes into the reality that we are one giant community organism. Isn't it critical to our liberation that we envision the possibility of healing ourselves and our perpetrators?

Our perpetrators didn't see us as full humans. They saw us as less than, separate than. They do not "deserve" our forgiveness, our kindness, our joy. It is not our responsibility to support them in their processes of healing. But I wonder how complete our healing can be if we see them (who are part of us) as only criminal, only perpetrator.

I am not beyond this yet. I don't know if there is a beyond, or if there should be. But I do wonder if I can truly heal without my perpetrator being healed as well.

L: *To envision that kind of healing is impossible without re-imagined communities. To engage in that kind of process is not just a question of forgiveness, but it's also a question of communal transformation. And it begins in conversation with one another. Like this. Like you and me.*

WHAT IF?

Perhaps, like me, you sometimes feel like everything inside of you is broken, like the pain has cut you so deeply that it defines you, like he or she or they scooped out everything beautiful and fine and strong within you and filled you up instead with burning bile, corrosive poison, endless shame. Sometimes it seems to me that the ache echoing from my father's twelve years of sadistic sexual abuse is so loud that I can hear nothing else, as if I am still drowning in his hate. But there is another voice within me, gentle and strong, and it says, *there is a place inside of you that the violence never touched, a place inside of you where no violence can ever touch.*

This might seem impossible to you, or very far away, or even like a dangerous lie. If it does seem that way, let it be instead a fairy tale, a hypothetical that you can hold briefly in your mind's eye as if it were a skittish dragonfly in your hand. What if this were true? How would that change you? Would it help? If not, let it fly away and turn the page.

Or try it on as if it were a new dress, sparkling and strange and perhaps not right for you. See how it feels against your skin, how it hangs on the curves of your body, these words: What if you were already whole? What if you were always already whole?

What if, hidden within you, there was a fire alive with heat and light and power? Your power. Your power to love, your power to change, your power to let even the most terrible pain change you in accordance with the rhythm of love?

Perhaps, like me, you sometimes shy away from these flames. I sometimes fear them because I know that to dance with fire I have to change, and the terrifying, exhilarating truth about change is that I never know exactly how I am going to transform or who I am going to be afterward. As someone whose trust was violated again and again, any loss of control, any surrender to unpredictable forces larger than myself is a challenge.

But there is a voice within me, playful and wise, that says, *you have the power to burn, the power to burn yourself, that which you thought was yourself, to let go of even the most deeply held stories you tell about yourself, to burn and burn and burn until all that remains is the clear, eternal flame of love.*

I find this fire by singing, by praying, by walking in the sun. In those moments when I let myself burn, inspiration flares up, illuminating hidden strengths and possibilities. The sense that I am powerful enough to change myself, my life, and my world blazes within me.

Emboldened by fire, the voice goes on: *What if, hidden within you, there were a wellspring of clear water bursting forth without ceasing? Water bubbling with the power to cleanse, to flow, to wash away?*

If and when you are ready, this water can pour into the places where you hold that burning bile, that corrosive poison, that endless shame. The water can—if you choose it—carry this pain and shame, rage and fear, to the surface of your mind.

In those moments when I make that choice, when the poison rises to my awareness, often my instinct is to clench up. But I try to breathe instead, breathe and open and let myself relax into the flow of the world—the rhythm of my legs walking, my chest rising and falling, my heart beating—my body always, endlessly in motion, the earth always holding me up, as steadfast and solid as my father never was. When I can manage this, the waters carry away the pain—I no longer have to hold it or guard it or carry it, any more than I have to hold the air in my lungs, the urine in my bladder. It becomes clear to me that the pain was never mine.

If and when you are ready, the waters within you can carry the pain up and out of you—the pain and fear, the bile, the poisonous shame. They carry all of this back to those it belongs to, to he or she or they who attempted to exorcise their own demons by injecting them into your innocent self.

Perhaps, like me, you will feel a pang of loss when this mass flows away from you and you feel suddenly, amazingly as empty as a balloon. I sometimes miss the pain and the shame, the rage and the fear that have been my steadfast companions for so long. I have mistaken them for pieces of myself and sometimes fear that letting go of them would be like losing an organ or a limb.

But a voice within me, loving and sure, says, *You are not your pain, your shame, your rage or your fear. You are not the poison he dumped into you. You are not the ancient shields you built to keep yourself safe in that terrible place. You are not who you were then.* When you open and breathe, fully inhabiting the present moment, you begin to see: you are this voice speaking to yourself, gentle and strong, playful and wise, loving and sure.

Shed a tear or two or many for what you are departing, but know that there is no need to tarry there, at the edge of yourself, the raw skin of a newly formed volcanic island. At any time you can return to the center, to that secret place deep within yourself, where the fire of your loving strength always burns true and hot; where the cleansing fountain leaps up into the air; where the air swims with the music of all your songs, sung and unsung, known and undiscovered.

Do you know the way to this place? Or have you yet to discover it? If you remember any of this letter—which I write as a map to find my own landscape of transformation and loving power, which I write as a spell to undo the curse laid on me by my father, which I write as the testimony of one who has been to this fire, who has felt this water flowing through my veins—if you remember any of this letter, remember this:

You will find your way to this place. You are already there.

Anne Averyt

THE HIKE TO AGAIN

Bone-weary I look to the mountain
smell the energy of conquest
hear the birds in meadow sing
of moving on ...

      Ripple of water
        coming back upon itself
  whispering "more"
    whispering "reach"

... and I breathe in the cold air
relax taut muscles I forgot
I had, my heart
saying,

      "Go on," "Climb,"
     "Learn to love again,"
  and I whisper *Now*
    and fly away ...

LIST OF CONTRIBUTORS AND BIOGRAPHIES

AAMINAH SHAKUR is a First Nations/Indigenous, queer, crip, poet, and artist. They are also a mother, a healer, and a birth/reproductive justice worker. Shakur's mixed-media arts combine words, images, paint, fiber arts and beadwork to explore love, gender, motherhood, spirituality, sexuality, history, borders, culture, privilege and oppression, abuse, freedom and revolution—and how all of these are interconnected. aaminahshakur.com.

ADRIENNE MAREE BROWN is a writer, artist, sci-fi scholar, facilitator, philosopher, and doula interested in healing. she believes we must transform ourselves to transform the world. she wrote her contribution for this collection in detroit.

AISHAH SHAHIDAH SIMMONS is a Black feminist lesbian filmmaker, writer, international lecturer, and activist. An incest and rape survivor, she is the producer, writer, and director of the internationally acclaimed, award-winning film *NO! The Rape Documentary*. She presently teaches in the Women's Studies and LGBT Studies programs at Temple

University, and was a Visiting Lecturer in the Department of Cinema and Media Studies at the University of Chicago. A member of the Editorial Collective of the online magazine *The Feminist Wire*, Aishah's cultural work and activism have been documented extensively in a wide range of media outlets including *The Root*, *Crisis*, *Forbes*, *Left of Black*, *In These Times*, *Ms.*, *Alternet*, *ColorLines*, *The Philadelphia Weekly*, National Public Radio, Pacifica Radio Network, and Black Entertainment Television.

ALEXIS PAULINE GUMBS is a queer black troublemaker, a black feminist love evangelist, a prayer poet priestess, and has a PhD in English, African and African-American Studies, and Women and Gender Studies from Duke University. Her scholarly work is published in *Obsidian, Symbiosis, Macomere, The Routledge Companion to Anglophone Literature, SIGNS, Feminist Collections, The Black Imagination, Mothering and Hip Hop Culture, The Business of Black Power,* and more. Alexis is the author of an acclaimed collection of poems *101 Things That Are Not True About the Most Famous Black Women Alive* and poetic work published in *Kweli, Vinyl, Backbone, Everyday Genius, Turning Wheel, UNFold, make/shift,* and more. Alexis is the founder of the *Eternal Summer of the Black Feminist Mind School* and *Brilliance Remastered* and is co-founder of the *Mobile Homecoming* project. Alexis was named one of *UTNE Reader's* 50 Visionaries Transforming the World in 2009, awarded a Too Sexy for 501-C3 trophy in 2011, was is one of the *Advocate's* top 40 under 40 featured in 2012 and is one of *GO Magazine's* 100 Women We Love in 2013.

ALLISON MCCARTHY is a freelance writer with a focus on intersectional feminism and social justice. Her work has been featured in print and online publications such as *The Guardian* (UK), *AlterNet*, *Ms.* (blog), *Bitch*, *Role/Reboot*, *Girlistic*, *Global Comment*, *The Feminist Wire*, *ColorsNW*, and *The Baltimore Review*, as well as in the anthologies *Robot Hearts: Twisted and True Tales of Seeking Love in the Digital Age* (Pinchback Press) and *21st Century Sex: Contemporary Issues in Pleasure and Safety* (Routledge). Allison's professional honors include being selected as a 2011 Editor's Favorite by *GOOD* magazine for her feature essay submission in the "Dealbreaker" series, as well as receiving an award from the 2007 Maryland Writers Association (MWA) Short Works Fiction Contest. She completed undergraduate work as a double-major in English (Honors) and Women's Studies at Goucher College in 2008 and graduated from the Master of Professional Writing program at Chatham University in 2013. She currently resides in the greater Washington, DC area.

AMITA Y. SWADHIN is an educator, activist and storyteller with NJ/NYC roots, now living and loving in Los Angeles. Her experiences as a queer woman of color, daughter of South Asian immigrants, and survivor of years of incestuous childhood rape and abuse inform her commitment to fighting institutional and interpersonal violence. Her favorite vehicles include popular education, oral history and poetry/essay writing, though she dabbles in journalism as a co-host of the weekly radio show *Flip the Script* on KPFK-LA. Amita is the co-creator and a former cast member of Secret Survivors, a theater and documentary project she conceived of for the off off-Broadway group Ping Chong & Co., featuring survivors of child sexual abuse telling their stories. She holds a Bachelor's degree from Georgetown University and an M.P.A. from NYU, where she was a Reynolds Fellow in Social Entrepreneurship. Her work has been featured in print on *The Feminist Wire*, *The Huffington Post*, and in the *Mujeres de Maiz* zine, *make/shift* magazine, and *Queering Sexual Violence* (Magnus Books, 2014).

AMY ERNST grew up outside of Washington, D.C. She received a bachelor's degree in Psychology from The Colorado College and is currently finishing her master's degree in International Relations at The University of Chicago. She worked for almost two years in North Kivu, Democratic Republic of Congo with both survivors and perpetrators of rape alongside Maman Marie Nzoli and her team. She volunteers as a Rape Crisis Counselor and Medical Advocate in Chicago, IL and is passionate about understanding the mechanisms behind sexual violence and working to prevent it in all forms.

ANA HEATON is a visual artist and writer living and working in the midwest. A disabled US Naval veteran, Ana is a full time student and single mother of two amazing girls.

ANDREA HARRIS teaches Women's Studies and English and was chosen as the "Instructor of the Year" at her university in 2011. She regularly teaches literature and media courses focusing on violence against women. She also co-founded a campus network of women who have survived violence. In appreciation for her service, Andrea received the 2010 Heart of Gold Award from the Lambda Chapter of the Eta Phi Beta Sorority. Andrea's published works include memoir pieces on her experiences as a survivor of rape and the joyful challenges of being a single mother and the parent of a child with autism.

ANGEL PROPPS is a multi-published author of erotica, horror, and poetry. When not out on road trip adventures with her butch partner and fellow author OB Hampton she splits her time between their homes in North Carolina and Florida. Lately she has taken up gardening and likens her garden to her life, sometimes things grow and sometimes they wither on the vine but the true beauty of it all lies in the soil from which it all grows.

ANNA SAINI has lived many lives as a political scientist, radical activist, and multi-media artist. She completed a B.A. and M.A. in Political Science from the University of Toronto and McMaster University respectively. She works as a community organizer on issues of equality in higher education, drug policy reform, prison abolition, women's abuse issues, police brutality, labor rights, and youth activism. Her writing appears in *Bitch Magazine*, *make/shift* magazine, various anthologies and journals, and her self-published poetry anthology *Colored Girls*. An interview with anna entitled "Sex Work and Feminism" appears in *Feminism for Real! Deconstructing the Academic Industrial Complex of Feminism*.

ANNE AVERYT is a survivor who has new life and meaning through writing and personal relationships.

She is a poet, essayist and commentator for Vermont Public Radio. Her poetry has appeared in *580 Split*, *Counterpoint*, *The Aurorean*, and *Mountain Troubadour*. She is 2nd place recipient of the Louise Wiehl Prize in poetry. She is currently experimenting with right-brain art and working with charcoal drawing.

ANNU SAINI is an ex-inmate, psychiatric and family violence survivor, and a poor and working class womyn of colour. She has been published in *make/shift* magazine, the poetry anthology *Coloured Girls*, *Asylum* magazine, and the book *Q? Y Art?*. She is a performance poet and conceptual artist. She is a lead producer, programmer and cohost of the show frequency feminisms. She lives happily in a community of people she loves.

frequencyfeminisms.com

BIRDY is a 35-year-old survivor. This writing has played a big part in her continued healing.

BROOKE BENOIT is a drop-out from the San Francisco Art Institute with a degree in Rhetoric from the University of Alaska in Anchorage. Currently she lives in a ram-packed earth house (think adobe) in the High Atlas Mountains of Morocco where she unschools her six children and is an editor at the international *SISTERS Magazine* (the magazine for fabulous Muslim women). Four of Brooke's babies have been born in the privacy and comfort of her own home. In 2012 when she was unable to find a homebirth-attending midwife in Casablanca, her sixth child was born at home with only the father attending to the birth. It was truly awesome.

BROWNFEMIPOWER is best described as a malinchista—a traitor to men, borders, and nation. She is a cook and a teacher and loves the smell of burning wood. She is a citizen of The Rust Belt.

DENISE SANTOMAURO served for five years as coordinator and facilitator of a Chicago-based child sexual abuse prevention program that used theater to educate children on sexual assault and abuse. Through this program, Denise has worked with hundreds of child survivors and their loved ones. While serving as coordinator, the program received numerous awards for partnering with outside agencies to combine sexual violence counseling and education services with theater performances. As a writer, Denise is currently completing edits on a young adult novel.

DESIRE VINCENT is somewhere saying, "Today is someday."

DORLA HARRIS, born of Jamaican decent, grew up in Southern Ontario, adopted into to a white family at the age of eight months. She is thankful for the diligence of her husband, who through searching was able to reunite her with her biological mother, and five half siblings. Her life is tremendously enriched by this connection to her roots. Dorla lives with her husband and two children in Vancouver BC. She works in the non-profit sector and continues to work towards a writing career.

HARRIET JAY is a mid-twenties white girl living in the Midwest. She works mostly as a paper-pusher in the government, but is occasionally exposed to spicier things.

INDIRA ALLEGRA is a poet and interdisciplinary artist exploring forms of queer intimacy, text, trauma, and racial identity through performance, video works, and handwoven textiles. A former fellow at both the Lambda Literary Foundation and Voice of Our Nations Arts Foundation (VONA), she is part of a segment on poetry in the Bay Area by BBC Radio 4. Indira has contributed work to *25 for 25: An Anthology of Works by 25 Outstanding Contemporary LGTB Authors*, *Yellow Medicine Review: A Journal of Indigenous Literature, Art and Thought*, *Sovereign Erotics: A Collection of Two Spirit Literature*, *Konch Magazine,* and *make/shift* magazine, among others. Indira has read and performed at events such as the National Queer Arts Festival, Litquake, the SF JAZZ Poetry Festival, and the Native American Poets Series at the de Young Museum. She performs regularly with Queer Rebels of the Harlem Renaissance and Mangos with Chili, and was a member of the artistic core of Sins Invalid in 2008. In 2012, Indira served as curator and creative director for Artists Against Rape, a biannual event hosted by San Francisco Women Against Rape. Her experimental videopoems *Blue Covers* and *Weep Willow: The Blues for Lady Day* have screened at film festivals internationally. In the Bay Area, Indira's textile works have shown at the Alter Space and College Avenue Galleries. She is currently completing her first collection of poems entitled *Indigo Season*.

indiraallegra.com

ISABELLA GITANA-WOOLF is a fierce Chicana Italian queer goddess, warrior, Mama, poet, artist, massage therapist, and incest survivor. She offers trauma aware massage and has developed a style of body centered trauma work for survivors of sexual and relationship violence. When she isn't working, she volunteers at the local Rape Crisis Center as a Rape Crisis Counselor Advocate. She is proud to tour with the Survivor Theatre Project in the award winning performance art piece she co-wrote and performs entitled "The World We Live In Is Not The World We Live In." It contains her original poetry and prose about how incest has affected her life. She can be reached at Isabella@SacredSpiralHealingArts.net.

JOAN CHEN is currently eating a pineapple bun in bed, feeling sweetened, sickened, full and torn. She has to stop (a rarity for her to stop in the middle of eating) to let these feelings roll through... and bloom into words...This is the first time her art has been published. This is the first time she has had to write a biographical blurb. Since she drew this Untitled image many years ago, she has learned so much about it—she could never have known. She would like to dedicate this experience to all those who have shared difficult stories with her, with grace, compassion and trust. Without them, she could never have known

jjoanchen.tumblr.com.

JUDITH STEVENSON is an incest survivor. She is currently an Assistant Professor of Anthropology in the Department of Human Development and Director of the Peace and Social Justice Program at California State University, Long Beach. Her research interests include grassroots political activism, human rights, feminist theory, globalization, and critical pedagogy in South Africa. Currently, she is conducting research in a rural community, exploring how communities protest human rights violations by the mining industry. In addition, she heads an international educational project called GlobaLinks2Peace, which partners schools in southern California with schools in South Africa via the internet.

JULIET NOVEMBER is a white working class femmetastic ladypants with a soft spot for prison/policing abolition, transformative justice, relationship building, and sex work organizing. Her work has been published in *The Revolution Starts At Home* and *The Walrus Magazine,* and she blogs at bornwhore.com. She currently lives on the occupied lands known as Toronto, Canada.

bornwhore.com

KATHLEEN AHERN is an educator and an activist in the queer and disability communities.

KYISHA WILLIAMS is a toronto born Black, queer, high femme, ma'star who is sex and sex work positive. She is an artist, primarily using written word, video, dance and collage. She has been organizing for over 10 years both locally and globally around violence and intersecting oppressions as they relate to colonialism, poverty, incarceration, gender, status, ability, sexuality and (sexual/mental) health.

LEAH LAKSHMI PIEPZNA-SAMARASINHA is a queer disabled Sri Lankan cis femme writer, performer, organizer and badass visionary healer. The author of the Lambda Award winning *Love Cake* and co-editor of *The Revolution Starts At Home:*

Confronting Intimate Violence in Activist Communities her work has appeared in the anthologies *Undoing Border Imperialism*, *Stay Solid!*, *Persistence*, *Yes Means Yes*, *Visible: A Femmethology*, *Homelands*, *Colonize This*, *We Don't Need Another Wave*, *Bitchfest*, *Without a Net*, *Dangerous Families*, *Brazen Femme*, *Femme*, and *A Girl's Guide to Taking Over The World*.

With Cherry Galette, she co-founded Mangos With Chili, North America's performance incubator for queer and trans people of color performance artists, and is a lead artist with Sins Invalid. In 2010 she was named one of the Feminist Press' "40 Feminists Under 40 Shaping the Future" and she is one of the the the 2013 Autostraddle Alternative Hot 105. She has taught, performed, and lectured across North America, Sri Lanka, and Australia and co-founded Toronto's Asian Arts Freedom School. Her first memoir, *Dirty River*, will be published by Deviant Type Press in winter 2013. She is also completing her third book of poetry, *Bodymap*, and a writer's manual, *Writing the World*, to be published by AK Press in 2014.

brownstargirl.org

MARIANNE KIRBY writes, edits, and polishes her nails in the land of year-round produce, Florida. She discusses fat, embodiment, class war, and nail polish at xoJane.com. Marianne is an unapologetic nerd with passion for *Star Trek* and the architecture of federal buildings. She is the coauthor of *Lessons from the Fat-o-sphere: Quit Dieting And Declare A Truce With Your Body*.

MAROULA BLADES is an Afro-British writer living in Berlin. The winner of the Erbacce Prize 2012, her first poetry collection *Blood Orange* is published by Erbacce-press. In April 2013, Maroula was awarded 2nd prize in the Leaf Art and Poetry Contest. Works have been published in the *Volume Magazine*, *Words with Jam*, *The Latin Heritage Foundation*, *Caribbean Writer*, *Peepal Tree,* and *Kaleidoscope Magazine,* and many other journals. Her poetry/music programme has been presented on several stages in Berlin. Maroula's poetry singles "Meta Stasis" and "Ms Betty" released by Havavision Records 2012 are available from iTunes and Amazon. Her new EP *Word Pulse* (Havavision Records, 2013) is also available as a download.

facebook.com/Poetrykitchen

MARY ZELINKA has been involved in the movement to end violence against women since 1980. She works at the Center Against Rape and Domestic Violence in Corvallis, Oregon, where every day she witnesses the remarkable strength and resiliency of survivors. Her writing has appeared in *CALYX*, *The Sun*, and *The Journey of Healing: Wisdom From Survivors of Sexual Abuse*.

MATTILDA BERNSTEIN SYCAMORE is most recently the author of a memoir, *The End of San Francisco* (City Lights 2013). She's also the author of two novels, *So Many Ways to Sleep Badly* (City Lights 2008) and *Pulling Taffy* (Suspect Thoughts 2003), and the editor of five nonfiction anthologies, including *Why Are Faggots So Afraid of Faggots?: Flaming Challenges to Masculinity, Objectification, and the Desire to Conform* (AK Press 2012), *Nobody Passes: Rejecting the Rules of Gender and Conformity* (Seal 2007), and *Dangerous*

Families: Queer Writing on Surviving (Haworth 2004).

mattildabernsteinsycamore.com

MELISSA DEY HASBROOK is a writer, artist, and community organizer based in Michigan. She integrates creative and healing arts, often partnering word art—especially poetry—with performance or visual art. Drawing upon life stories including experience as a survivor, Melissa engages The Personal as a portal for building community, artistic inspiration, and spiritual growth. Most recently, her projects include an artist's book, *The Vision Journal*, a series with workshops and exhibits entitled "Words & Afterwords," and a visually-designed poetry collection *Circle...Home*. She may be reached for invitation at MelissaHasbrook@gmail.com.

deyofthephoenix.com

MELISSA GORDON is a poet, former teacher, love-bug, soul sister, music lover, survivor and firestarter living and working in southern Connecticut. She is currently working on her first chapbook of poetry and is an editor for rising young poets. She believes in the power of the arts to change everything. Her poems have been featured in national literary magazines. Her heart and the ring finger on her left hand belong to T.

MIA MINGUS is a writer, community educator and organizer working for disability justice and transformative justice responses to child sexual abuse. She identifies as a queer physically disabled Korean woman transracial and transnational adoptee, born in

Korea, raised in the Caribbean, nurtured in the South and now living on the west coast. She works for community, interdependency and home for all of us, not just some of us, and longs for a world where disabled children can live free of violence, with dignity and love. As her work for liberation evolves and deepens, her roots remain firmly planted in ending sexual violence. Her work on disability justice has been cited and used in numerous texts and events around the world.

leavingevidence.wordpress.com.

MICHELLE OVALLE is a New Jersey poet who holds an MFA from Drew University. Her poems and book reviews have appeared in or are forthcoming in several journals, including *The Stillwater Review*, *Painted Bride Quarterly*, A*danna Literary Journal*, and *OVS Magazine*. She currently teaches grammar and literature at a local community college. When not writing or teaching, Michelle enjoys photography, mosh pits, and red dresses.

PREMALA MATTHEN is a freelance writer and activist living in Vancouver, British Columbia.

REBECCA WYLLIE DE ECHEVERRIA crafts stories that explore peoples' behavior and link them to the larger system of privilege and oppression. She spends her free time cooking, sailing small boats, and riding her non-fixey bicycle.

RENÉE MARTIN is the executive editor of the blog *Womanist Musings* and co-creator of the blog *Fangs for the Fantasy*. Her writing has appeared in T*he*

Guardian (UK), *Global Comment*, *GOOD*, *theGrio*, *Loop21,* and *Clutch*, as well as *Ms.* magazine's blog. Her work has been discussed on CNN, CBC/Radio-Canada, and NPR. Her round-table contributions to "Mothers of Intention: Five Bloggers on Race and Erasure in the Mommy Blogosphere" were published both online and in the fall 2011 issue of *Bitch*. Her essay "Confronting Hyper-Sexuality in the Black Community" was published in Jessica Yee's anthology *Sex Ed and Youth: Colonization, Sexuality, and Communities of Colour* (Canadian Centre for Policy Alternatives). In between chasing her lovely two children around and feeding the dog, much of her work is dedicated to discussing everyday issues from a social justice perspective.

RIVER WILLOW FAGAN is a genderqueer writer who grew up in Southeastern Michigan. Their short stories have appeared in *Fantasy Magazine* and *The Year's Best Science Fiction and Fantasy 2011*. Two of their essays are in the anthologies *Queering Sexual Violence* and *Why Are Faggots So Afraid of Faggots?: Flaming Challenges to Masculinity, Objectification and the Desire to Conform.*

SARA DURNAN grew up in upstate New York. The second youngest of eight children, she followed in her siblings' footsteps as she traveled the world. She has lived and studied in Costa Rica, Italy, Peru and Spain. She holds degrees in both Business and Spanish Language and Literature. She currently resides in Hungary where she teaches elementary school. She feels forever indebted to her family, friends and Barbara from Victims Information Bureau of Suffolk

County (VIBS). Without the gift of their unending love and support, she would not be where she is today.

SARAH CASH is a sensualist who refuses to wear a watch as she believes in living in the moment. She admires those with decisive walks because she's a meandering sort. She has experienced failure before success. She defines success for herself. She believes in: slow dancing in the kitchen to the Drifters, writing inscriptions in books given as gifts, good conversation, comfortable silences, nights like jazz, the continued applicability of the Civil Rights Movement, and peanut butter pie. She may be found facing the world with the perfect tube of lipstick and a lot of sass.

SHALA BENNETT is a soul on a quest to understand the reasons why. With her goal in mind she's explored art, history, technology. And life has never stopped offering opportunities for her to learn more and more.

SHANNA KATZ, M.Ed ACS, is a sexuality educator, board certified sexologist, and author based in the Southwest. As a queer femme with disabilities, she works to provide accessible sex education and support to the LGBTQ, PWD, poly, and other frequently ignored, marginalized, and/or fetishized communities. She lives with her partner and their three (rescued) kitties, and enjoys British mystery novels, dialogue around social justice and cupcakes.

ShannaKatz.com and @shanna_katz

SOFIA ROSE SMITH is a femme of color, magic-maker, freedom dreamer and poet. She is from Los

Angeles, the land her family migrated to 100 years ago. Sofia believes in green leaves and sunlight, wind through our hair, rustling trees, gateways, circles, arches, mountains, friends, love, the healing power of words, and our tongues. She is grateful to be part of this sacred offering of poems, tears, and wisdom, like a bowl of water that we drink from together, in ceremony.

When not scribbling pieces of her soul on paper, **SUMAYYAH TALIBAH** is a wife, mother, and avid reader. Her work can be found in *Liberated Muse Volume 1: How I Freed My Soul, Liberated Muse Volume 2: Betrayal Wears a Pretty Face*, and several zines.
SumayyahSaidSo.com

SYDETTE HARRY is a writer singer blogger problem NYC born by way of the Guyana. Writing as Blackamazon, she has started boycotts but she is most proud of making her fellow beautiful girls of every color feel not alone and thankful they have done the same for her by SPEAK!ing. She continues to blog at *Having Read The Fine Print* (guyaneseterror. blogspot.com) and *Blackamazon Is Too Much* (blackamazon.tumblr.com), theorize heavily, write the first play of Salt&Rice Productions, apply for a PHD, and try to fall in love a little bit more every day.

VIANNAH E. DUNCAN is an author, poet, editor, human.
duncanheights.com.

ZÖE FLOWERS is a Reiki Master, actress, poet, and playwright. Her poetry can be found in anthologies:

Stand Our Ground Poems for Trayvon Martin and Marissa Alexander, The Women Writers in Bloom Anthology, and several online journals. Zoë is also the author of *Dirty Laundry: Women of Color Speak up about Dating & Domestic Violence* and a meditation CD entitled, *Balance-An Evening Meditation for Activists, Advocates and Helping Professionals.* Zoë is also the founder of Highest Good Consulting (HGC). HGC provides a wide range of trainings and project management in the fields of domestic violence, child abuse, and sexual assault. HGC also coordinates wellness retreats for advocates and community members. Zoë frequently speaks nationally and has spoken internationally on the issue of domestic violence, has appeared on National Public Radio, and makes her living as a healer and teaching artist.

ABOUT AK PRESS

AK Press is one of the world's largest and most productive anarchist publishing houses. We're entirely worker-run and democratically managed. We operate without a corporate structure—no boss, no managers, no bullshit. We publish close to twenty books every year, and distribute thousands of other titles published by other like-minded independent presses from around the globe.

The Friends of AK program is a way that you can directly contribute to the continued existence of AK Press, and ensure that we're able to keep publishing great books just like this one! Friends pay $25 a month directly into our publishing account ($30 for Canada, $35 for international), and receive a copy of every book AK Press publishes for the duration of their membership! Friends also receive a discount on anything they order from our website or buy at a table: 50% on AK titles, and 20% on everything else. We've also added a new Friends of AK ebook program: $15 a month gets you an electronic copy of every book we publish for the duration of your membership. Combine it with a print subscription, too!

There's great stuff in the works—so sign up now to become a Friend of AK Press, and let the presses roll!

Email friendsofak@akpress.org for more info, or visit the Friends of AK Press website:
www.akpress.org/programs/friendsofak